Cherie Whiting is a pioneer. She has honed her holistic approach to leadership during a time when women leaders were few and far between. While many woman leaders of that era tried to "out testosterone" their male colleagues, Cherie recognized the unique strengths women bring to the leadership role. Cherie generously shares her "secret sauce" of success that is applicable not only for women leaders but all leaders who wish to rise above average performance to achieve personal and business excellence."

—Dottie Deremo, President and CEO,
Hospice of Michigan

Cherie Whiting is "The Real Deal" A highly successful CEO, one of the true entrepreneurs I have met, a bundle of enthusiasm and energy as well as a dedicated mother and wife. She is one of the most effective leaders I have met and she is adored by those who work for her. In her book, she shares her wealth of knowledge and experience. Cherie has created a book that is a rallying cry for women leaders to take charge of their destiny and she gives them the tools to accomplish it!"

—Robert Milewski
Senior Vice President, Operations
and Health Care Value
Blue Cross Blue Shield of Michigan

Cherie Whiting is a breath of fresh air! She focuses on the *realities* of leadership and creating a successful business. She inspires all around her by showing that you CAN create the culture you want in your business and still hit your targets. Cherie is a savvy business woman who empowers others to reach their personal best and in turn, they strengthen her companies. Entrepreneurs, both men and women, can take Cherie's experiences and begin designing what they really want their business to be like. Her book is powerful . . . just wait until you hear her speak!

—Kristina Marshall
President & CEO, Winning Futures
Author of youth workbooks:
Road to Success and Achieving Success

Cherie gives her formula for HR success that all organizations, no matter what their size, would do well to notice!

—Joni C. Nelson
Vice President Human Resources
Ilitch Holdings, Inc.

HELLO SUCCESS!

Blessings as you create
your own world.

Cheri

DR. CHERIE WHITING

Published by Tate Publishing & Enterprises, LLC
127 E. Trade Center Terrace | Mustang, Oklahoma 73064 USA
1.888.361.9473 | www.tatepublishing.com

Tate Publishing is committed to excellence in the publishing industry. The company reflects the philosophy established by the founders, based on Psalm 68:11,
"The Lord gave the word and great was the company of those who published it."

Cover design by Kellie Vincent
Interior design by Christina Hicks
Title by Lauren Bartlett

Published in the United States of America

ISBN: 978-1-61346-445-8
1. Business & Economics / Women in Business
2. Business & Economics / Leadership
11.08.31

Dedication

This book is dedicated to every little girl, no matter what her age, who only awaits the knowledge that she can do anything she dreams of and far more.

Acknowledgement

I would like to acknowledge my mother, Donna Jean Cadle Chartier, who mothered me and mentored me and taught me everything I really needed to know in order to live a full and successful life. And I thank her especially for perhaps the greatest advice she ever gave me: Get Your Education, You Can Get Married Anytime! Thanks Momma–I Love You!

Table of Contents

Chapter One: The World for Women

What does the world for women today look like in the United States? *Time* magazine presented a special report in its October 26, 2009, issue entitled "The State of the American Woman." Their conclusion was that women are more powerful yet less happy. They weren't sure why, however, considering all the advances women have made since they ran a similar report in 1970. I read the article at a ten-minute oil change place, and just reading the article was so upsetting that I'm afraid the poor oil change guy might have mistaken my glares as a reflection on him. Why aren't women happy? Amidst all the great statistics on how far we have come, there was that one statistic in the article that jumped off the page at me: women only make seventy-seven cents on the dollar for doing a comparable job as a man! The ending statement that this is no longer a man's world rang quite hollow. What struck me was how far we haven't come . . .

In 1975, while immersed in my studies at Andrews University, I read a statistic that women made sixty-two cents on the dollar compared to a man in a similar job. When I relayed what I thought was this shocking piece of news to my father, he replied that, yes, that was right. I asked him, "Why would a man make more money than a woman for doing the exact same job?" His answer was that a man had a family to support, so he should make more. I said it again—a man should make more money for the exact same job a woman was doing because he has a family to support? I asked then, "Should a man make more money the more children he has?" My dad didn't answer, and I knew that at least he paused to think about the whole idea. It was my first realization that the workplace might not be a just place.

However, I should have noticed the warning signs. Growing up on a horse farm, I did notice that my brothers got a paycheck for working in the farming and excavating business while my sister and I worked equally hard in the house, yard, and barn for no pay. All of our needs were provided for; that certainly wasn't the issue. But the message was clear: what we did, did not warrant pay. That nagging thought that I wasn't worth the pay would plague me for many years to come until I was able to examine the origin of the thought and realize that it was not valid.

It boggled my mind then and continues to boggle it today that some people believe, and in fact a lot of people believe, that a man may perform a job better simply because of his gender. Some people, many people, and even people within my own family believe it today, and it is almost incomprehensible to me.

That conversation with my dad 30 years ago burned into my memory. It was my introduction to the inequities experienced by women in the workplace. As a nurse, where women dominate the profession, the inequities were not so apparent for a time though I became acutely aware that the people in the executive offices (excepting the secretaries) were usually men. This even applied to the nurse executives. It was when I ventured out to start my own business that I began to experience discrimination because of my gender and age. I was overlooked and underestimated when I made marketing calls and sought financing. But every day I got up and kept trying, and over the next twenty-five years I built a substantial company, winning awards and honors along the way. Not having a business degree, I built my companies with my own values and ideas and did what made sense to me. In time, gender didn't really seem to be much of an issue any longer. Of course, the age concern eventually resolved itself. During this time my husband and I were raising three children—a daughter, born first, and two sons. I knew that the moment my sons were born they had an advantage over my daughter just because they were born white males. For that reason and in my own effort to change thinking regarding women, I carefully taught my philosophy on women to my children and especially my daughter. I remember times we spent together role-playing the life I wanted her to be able to live if she so chose. With her stuffed Kermit Frog and Miss Piggy, we would pretend that Miss Piggy went off to work in her executive job and Kermit stayed home with the kids. My daughter was involved in my businesses from an early age, acting as a receptionist at fifteen. She knew a lot about my struggles growing a business. When she reached young womanhood, I remember the day I proudly told her that the world had changed in those twenty-some years and would be a kinder and gentler place for her to work with equity.

In the early years of growing my business, I became partners with a local hospital, which provided me with much-needed capital and referrals. In the twenty years I worked with the hospital, I worked in large part with men who had a respect for women. About twenty years into the venture, I sold the remaining stock to the hospital I had partnered with and stayed on as CEO. Even in this capacity I was able to maintain the company as I had built it while still being able to operate separately from the hospital and its bureaucracy. However, the hospital experienced financial problems and was forced to merge with a hospital system. This, of course, merged my company as well. The hospital system owned a homecare company larger than mine, and I was quite aware that they probably wouldn't need two CEOs. Shortly after the merger, the CEO position for the larger home care company became available when their existing CEO, a woman about my age, was fired. Thrilled, I expected my move into that position to be natural. One of the hospital board members that I had worked with for many years called me to let me know about a conversation he had just had with the system CEO about me and the open position. He wanted me to know that, based on that conversation, he didn't think I was going to be given the new position. It seems I didn't fit the "criteria" of what they were looking for. Was it because I didn't have credentials? With a PhD in leadership, a twenty-three-year track record of starting and growing companies, and awards over the years that included Michigan's Entrepreneur of the Year and Detroit Crain's 40 under 40, I felt quite sure it wasn't for a lack of credentials. I had been warned that the system was notorious for not letting women get ahead and that the hospital CEO hired people who "looked like him." That would be a white male between the ages of forty-five and fifty-five, and it would really help if an applicant was Italian and Catholic.

I applied for the position anyway. A national recruiter had been hired to find that perfect person for the job. Finally the day arrived for my screening interview with him. Our conversation started off with questions about what kind of car I drove (a big issue when you live in Michigan), and it didn't take long to get to religion. When he asked my religion and learned I was a member of a fundamentalist protestant religion, he asked me if that wasn't just about as far from Catholicism as you could get. The conversation went downhill from there. As much as I endeavored to sell him on what I could do for the organization, the conversation didn't get too far in that direction. When I walked to my car after that screening interview, it was with a sinking heart. Not long after, I received an e-mail from the system's corporate office proudly announcing the selection of the homecare agency's new CEO—a white male around fifty-five years old.

It was then that it struck me that the world really hadn't changed at all. What had happened in those twenty-three years since I had started my companies was that I had created my own world, and it "felt" like the world had changed. I had created my own reality.

About this time I read an article in *The Harvard Business Review* called "Women and the Labyrinth of Leadership" by Alice Eagly and Linda Carli. This article made several good points, a few that I will mention here. First of all, there really isn't a glass ceiling keeping women from the top because few make it to the top to even knock on that ceiling. To be specific, only 6 percent of executive positions with Fortune 500 companies are held by women, and only 2 percent of the CEOs are women. Only 15 percent of the boards of directors have women holding seats. It's not that women hit a glass ceiling; it's that women get lost and dropped along the labyrinth of leadership and never make it close enough to the top to hit a ceiling. Women are in a no-win situation as leaders; meaning that they aren't respected by men if they manage with characteristics that are identified as womanly attributes, and men are uncomfortable and offended if a woman, in essence, manages like a man. In addition, as women continue to do a majority of the child rearing, women lose valuable opportunities when they drop out of the workplace to have babies, and they miss after-hour networking opportunities because they're managing their homes. So, in a nutshell, women lag behind men because of a continuing prejudice against women in leadership because a woman's leadership style remains in question, because of demands of family life and insufficient time and opportunity to network.

So I took a look at the statistics: According to www.statistics.gov, the gender pay gap is narrowing, but there remains a 12.6 percent gap between men and women. This is just a median measurement of all jobs and doesn't address comparable jobs. According to the report, women make seventy-four cents on the dollar for a comparable job done by a man. In thirty years, women have gained twelve cents. At that rate of improvement, I can't live long enough to see parity for women in the workplace. With lack of parity in pay compounded by the fact that women scraping their way to the top of the corporate ladder are in a no-win situation, I came to my own conclusion, that in order to live in a world fulfilling to me, I would again need to build my own world. I again called my daughter, this time to say, "Honey, I was wrong. It isn't a new world of equity for women, but that doesn't matter; you can build your own world, just like I did. You can create the world you want to live in. In fact, you *must* create your own world."

So when that new CEO came in and a year later when my contract was not renewed and I was sent on my way, I set out to again create a world for myself, as I wanted it to be. And one day, on my way to my new world, as I was driving along I-94, it struck me that I needed to tell women how I created that world of mine. I needed to write a book that equips and inspires women to create their own worlds. You see, women in leadership is one of my greatest passions. I want to help women in any way that I can. So here is the book on how to create your own world.

Now, if you're skeptical I want you to think a minute about it, and you'll know that it's true and possible. Mike Vance, author of the popular book *Think Out of the Box*, told a story at a conference I was attending of how he created his own world within his sleeping bag while serving during the Korean War. He also tells the story in his book *Think Out of the Box*, which I will retell here. He was stationed not far from the enemy lines where they spent most of their time in trenches. They slept in sleeping bags within these trenches and lived in a state of terror because infiltrators would burst upon them, usually at night, and kill them in their sleeping bags. Many of Vance's buddies had been killed in such a way. The soldiers spent a lot of time in their sleeping bags, trying to stay as warm as possible in a freezing environment where frostbite was common. The sleeping bags, while giving some sense of security, were also dark cold places where their lives seemed too close in a way, as they could hear themselves breathing and had nothing but their terrifying thoughts to occupy their time. One day Vance decided he had to change his environment—to enrich it. He just couldn't stand it the way it was any longer. He started to create a virtual world for himself within his sleeping bag. He scavenged the area until he found discarded wooden ammo boxes that he used to build a little structure to form his sleeping bag into a little room even though this room was really only from the waist up. He covered the walls with paper to create storyboards where he could draw pictures he had in his mind. He created lighting by taping flashlights to improvised tent poles. He used his army hand warmers fueled with cigarette lighter fluid to form a makeshift potbellied stove, which made his "room" so warm sometimes that he had to zip open the bag to let in some cool air. He devised a concoction of coffee and sugar that he dipped his badly tasting rations in to make them more palatable, which he would nibble on while drawing in his warm, lighted room. He acquired a radio in which he could tune in classical music from the Far East Command radio station. He used a walkie talkie to communicate with other guys. Of course, this virtual room also had pictures from home, news clippings, and other items that would make his environment happier. Then to increase his security he devised "alerts" with wire and cans that would rattle if someone tried to sneak in. Because of his example, guys started to create their own "bag environments" in his unit, and this concept had a marked impact on the morale of the soldiers as times got even tougher.

One of the biggest advantages of creating our own world that is friendly to women is that we can influence and affect the lives of those within our world for the better. As Mike Vance changed his life and those lives around him, so can you change lives within your sphere of influence for the better. And at the end of the day, or really the end of a life, that may be the most important thing you have accomplished. And a very worthy accomplishment it is as well.

Albert Einstein said that "reality is an illusion, albeit a persistent one." We can create our own reality and world, or we can passively let the world create what we know as our reality. In this book we will discuss mostly building a world in the business world. For me, that world is built within the confines of businesses I start and own. Some of you aren't comfortable with building your own business, or it just isn't what you desire to fulfill your life. In that case, you will need to build your own world within the confines of the larger world that might not be under your control. But regardless, you and I and our daughters and granddaughters will be better served by creating our own worlds within the world in which we live. We must make our own worlds, and in the pages ahead I will tell you how I did that, and how you can too. It is a world in which life is as you want it to be. But there's one thing you need to know right now: don't expect men to "get it" and understand what you're doing, and don't expect a lot of women to "get it" either. My husband understands because in twenty-five years of living with me, he's watched everything unfold. He's seen what I've accomplished, what I've been up against, and rejoiced with me along the way. Just a few weeks ago, I was invited to join a friend for dinner and meet two interesting men CEOs who do strategic thinking and educating with top management staff. During that dinner we discussed the needs of women in leadership positions to have education and support and to sometimes get those things separate from men because of their distinct and separate concerns and issues. While one of the men had heard that need from women CEOs he knew, neither one could really acknowledge that there is in fact a difficulty for women in leadership and that those women in top leadership positions have to play the men's game to get ahead and, in fact, make men comfortable with them. Men as a whole just don't "get it" in regards to women in leadership, and at this point, I would suggest that you just don't expect them to. It will save frustration for you if you don't. And you really can't blame them for not getting it. After all, it's so different from their world. Their reality is just different.

I went back again to that *Time* magazine article that bothered me so to see what I had missed. Why would these women authors close their article with the following: "It's no longer a man's world. Nor is it a woman's nation. It's a cooperative, with bylaws under constant negotiation and expectations that profits be equally shared"? I looked at the beginning of the magazine and discovered, to my delight, that the Chairman and CEO is indeed a woman. That just confirmed my premise. The reality of the world of these *Time* authors is just as they write. In their reality it doesn't seem to be a man's world any longer. Well, if I did it in the past and they're doing it now, then we all can do it, can't we? We certainly can. Let's get started!

Chapter Two: Beginning the World

The snow was gently falling against the windshield as I drove to the home of my first patient. It was Christmas Eve, and already the sun was starting to set. I was a little nervous, and everything felt just surreal. I shouldn't be nervous; this first patient I was going to visit was my grandmother, but today was different. I wasn't visiting her just as her granddaughter, but also as her nurse. And she wasn't just any patient; she was the first patient of my new company, Personal Home Care.

Maybe this evening felt surreal because all had seemed that way for the last fifty-four days. Fifty-five days ago, I was living the ordinary life of a nurse educator. Fifty-five days ago I was a newlywed, married to a man living an ordinary life. But fifty-four days ago, that had changed. When I went into work on November 1, 1984, it was a cheerful, ordinary day as I set about educating nurses in the intensive care unit of a local hospital. It was actually sort of a high day because the night before, the hospital aired its new television commercial in which I had a small speaking part. Shortly after getting to my office, I received a call that the director of nursing wanted to see me. She and I had a great relationship, and I wasn't worried at the call, but as soon as I sat down in her office, I knew something was wrong. She was stern and serious. She told me that they had learned that I was starting a home care company and hiring away hospital staff. I could write a letter of resignation or be fired. I told her it wasn't true, but there would be no discussion. She handed me a blank sheet of paper and a pen. I wrote my one-line resignation. A security guard stepped into the room and walked me to my desk where I gathered my few belongings, and he walked me down the hall, outside the building, and into the parking garage to my car. There he stood, watching me until I drove off the hospital grounds. I managed to contain my tears until I turned onto the avenue running alongside the hospital. The tears came slowly at first, but I was sobbing by the time I reached the expressway. I tried to grasp what had happened. Someone had told the administration that I was starting my own company. The truth was that I had been dreaming of starting a company and had attended a little seminar on what being in home care was like, but I hadn't taken that wish and dream to anything real. I was a newlywed, and we didn't have any extra money. We'd only been married seven months and were renting a house. We hardly had enough money to support ourselves, much less hire anyone else. It was a long drive home, trying to see through my tears. As soon as I got home, I called my husband and then my dad. In about half an hour, they were there. I remember putting my head down at the table and sobbing and sobbing. You see, you didn't get fired in my family. We were raised to work and to work hard and to have done something to get fired was unconscionable. This was a case of shame and humiliation. But, much to my relief, there were no stern words of reprisal from my dad. He listened to my story, and then he said, “Well, you wanted to start a home care company. Here’s your chance. Stop crying over spilled milk. I’ll give you five thousand dollars to get started.” Quickly the tears stopped, and the imagination started to work. We discussed start-up details. My dad was an entrepreneur, who, with my mother started several companies. Neither had an education past high school, yet they had been extremely successful. He offered me some advice that day, which was to be the wisest business advice I’ve ever received. First of all we discussed location of office, and my dad said that I needed a real office. I needed to look professional and legitimate. Secondly, he said I’d need to find a good lawyer and a good accountant and that I should use these professionals as tools but never let them make decisions for me. Just use their advice to make my own decisions. With that advice given and received, we hopped in his pickup and went to look for office space.

We found office space in downtown New Baltimore. Downtown New Baltimore, Michigan consists of one street three city blocks long. I found a nice looking three hundred fifty-square-foot office in the first block, and I signed the lease that afternoon. It was made out in my name—we didn't have a company name yet! In a few short hours, I went from devastation and shame, to the thrill of starting a new business. I went from an eight-hour-a-day job with a salary to working sixteen to seventeen hours a day for no pay! I went from sitting at home, waiting for my husband to come home and worrying about the spot on the couch to not noticing what time it was at all, much less if there was a spot on the couch. Later I would realize that without that firing from my job, I might never have started my business. God had given me a nudge. And it would not be the last nudge that turned into great things.

The first work was to envision the company. I wanted the name to represent us and what we wanted to do. It was during that reflection that I thought of the name Personal Home Care of Michigan. We were going to give care with the personal touch. We would care for and about the individual and their needs. One of the reasons I thought about going into home care was because about this time, my grandmother was starting to need care to remain at home. I stood on the periphery as I watched her children wondering what to do. Grandma wanted to stay home with my grandfather more than anything. I knew that if she needed help to stay at home there must be thousands of grandmas and grandpas, moms and dads, and children who needed help to stay at home. It was with the thought of my grandmother that I started to form all policies and practices for this new company. You see, she wasn't just any grandma. She was the grandma you envision when you hear, "Over the river and through the woods, to Grandmother's house we go." When I think of my grandma, I think of her when I was a little girl and would visit her at her home at their riding stables. When I would come into the house and into Grandma's kitchen, she would always be standing there with one of those aprons on that had a bib and two big pockets in the front. She would always have a jar of windmill cookies on her counter, and if I was lucky enough to get to spend the night with Grandma and Grandpa, she would have a cinnamon fry donut and orange and grapefruit sections for me to eat in the morning. How I loved my grandma, and I wanted a company that would care for her as she deserved to be cared for. So, the name Personal Home Care was born with the vision that it would serve patients all over Michigan, and we would deliver excellent care with the personal touch. My husband, Bill, worked on the logo and brochure while I worked on what we would have to do to be approved by Medicare to take care of patients.

Taking care of patients under Medicare meant having policies and procedures in place to meet all of their conditions of participation. We needed to know in depth exactly how we would handle clinical as well as employee issues. To me, this was a matter of meshing the government requirements with common sense. As you can imagine, those two items are not necessarily easily meshed, as the government has a tendency to be redundant. However, the writing of the clinical policies was accomplished. At the time, writing policies and procedures seemed unnecessary and something only to be done to satisfy the Medicare program. I learned in time that policies and procedures give you a consistent guide for how to operate your business. It provides a reference for any employee to use and standardization for how you will do things on a day-to-day basis.

Policies and procedures are especially important for human resource or, as I like to call it, talent resource management. You especially want to be consistent with your talent resources; it will save you headaches and legal hassles later. The job I was fired from before starting Personal Home Care had the worst management environment that I had ever worked in. When I started making my personnel policies, I did exactly the opposite of what I had seen practiced. For instance, the VP of nursing hid in the stairwells and listened in on conversations, and she or someone else would sometimes look through our garbage at night. There was at least one administrative assistant spying to try to catch us doing something wrong. I decided that I would expect that everyone would give me their best efforts. We wouldn't have time clocks or spend needless time tracking minutes. I came up with my formula for successful people management. I expected people to do their best every day, and every day I thanked someone for something that they did. I let the staff know that I appreciated them, and we took pause to celebrate every little thing that we could, big or small. But I'm getting a little ahead of myself because at this point I was the only employee. However, when you're dreaming for the future, you have to dream big like everybody is already there. And I have to tell you that through the years, I expected great things from people, and they delivered it to me at least 95 percent of the time.

We finished our logo and put together a brochure. We put policies and procedures together. We bought furniture and put it into our little three hundred fifty-square-foot office. On Sundays we would go into the office and rearrange the furniture, clean, and look around with the expectation of what would be coming. I needed two things: patients and staff, and I needed them at the same time. I talked with my grandpa about caring for Grandma. He came up with the idea that he would advance me cash with which to operate, and in turn I charged him at cost. It was a nice arrangement for starting. Grandma needed care that a home care aide would give; that is, she needed help with bathing and personal hygiene, help getting meals prepared, and supervision and company so that my Grandpa could get out and keep his activities going. I started looking for home care aides by putting an ad in the paper. When I started interviewing those potential aides, I would look across the interview table at them and ask myself, "Is this person good enough to take care of my grandma?" It was a pretty tough test to pass, but some did. And so it was on that Christmas Eve that I opened the case of my very first patient, my grandmother.

When you're building your own world and wanting to start a new business, you can look at established products and services, or you can look for something new. I found a new opportunity: a cottage industry just finding its wings. You can find a new opportunity too—keep your eyes open to needs that aren't being met. I saw my opportunity when my grandma needed help to stay at home. It matched my skills as a nurse and my desire to be in business for myself. As a nurse, caring for people had been my passion, and I found an opportunity that would follow that passion. Whatever you decide to do, whatever opportunity you decide to pursue, it should follow your passion. Sometimes it's only the passion for what you're doing that keeps you going. Besides, life is much too short to spend it making a living or spending most of your time doing something that you aren't passionate about.

The initial advice I received from my father was the best business advice I ever received. Find good counselors in an accountant and attorney, but always make your own decisions. They are not in your business and should only be used as tools for you to operate your own business. In addition, your offices and person should always look professional. This increases credibility. It might be tempting to spend less money and work out of your home, but if yours is a business in which clients or employees will visit your premises, make sure it looks the part. And make sure you look the part too; whatever the image is of the business you start, you should personify that image.

Chapter Three: Defining the World

That thrill of having my first patient and the awe of the responsibility of caring for someone I loved as much as my grandmother came together in one moment that I will never forget. I remember the exact feeling, the look of the snow as it hit the windshield, and exactly the bend in the road where I was on the road to Grandma's house. My grandma needed home care aides to care for her. I put ads out in the newspaper, looking for staff to care for Grandma. Only a select few were hired because each person had to be the best to care for my precious grandma.

When I happily received a referral for my second patient and I was interviewing staff to care for him, I looked across the interview table from those potential employees, and all of a sudden it hit me: if this person wasn't good enough to care for my grandma, then they shouldn't care for anyone's grandma or grandpa. It not only became our benchmark for hiring staff from that time forward, but it also began to really define our world and who we would become. We became known as the agency started for a grandmother and that treated each patient as if they were their grandmother. Each employee either touched somebody who was receiving care or touched somebody that touched someone else giving care. So with something as simple as benchmarking how we would care for everyone within our sphere of influence, we defined who we were in such an enormous way that the behaviors of every employee was affected. Those behaviors, in turn, determined quality and customer service, and it made people feel special about what they were doing.

Beside the home care aides who I had hired to care for Grandma, I was the only employee. I made marketing calls, interviewed, oriented staff and worked on obtaining Medicare certification. One day when I was making marketing calls, I called on a doctor's office in a small town. It was a shabby office, and the curtains were askew in the windows. I wouldn't have dreamed that a week after making the call I would receive a referral. It was to take care of a patient twenty-four hours a day, seven days a week, and they would be paying privately. I learned from that marketing call that I should never underestimate where a referral might originate from. I never would have guessed that the shabby little office would produce such a great referral.

Taking care of what are termed "private duty" patients is one type of home care. In private duty we care for people from four hours to twenty-four hours a day. The Medicare side of home care is the traditional visits made by nurses, aides, and therapists. Besides having policies and procedures in place that conform to the government's conditions of participation, before a Medicare surveyor will come out and review your agency for compliance with the program, you have to have cared for eight patients. These are patients you will never receive payment for, which isn't too bad, however the real difficulty is in obtaining those eight patients in the first place. I started marketing area hospitals and doctor offices to try to obtain those eight patients. The trouble came because most hospitals and offices require that you are Medicare certified to ensure you have a quality they can count on. You have to have seen patients to become certified, but they won't give you patients until you are! It was a frustrating experience. I was eventually able to procure those eight patients, but it took a lot of marketing calls, and finally begging, to get those patients, and that was with one of the patients being my grandmother and the other my mother-in-law! Finally, we were scheduled to be surveyed by the Michigan Department of Public Health in cooperation with the Medicare program to see if we met the conditions to become a Medicare provider. It was April 2, 1985. I was fresh-faced and nervous, and the surveyor was very kind. Her name was Carolyn Connelley. Carolyn was later to become director of that department and left a great legacy behind her when she succumbed to cancer almost twenty years later. I will never forget her kindness to me. She reviewed our operations and visited patients in their homes and recommended that we become Medicare certified. And although it would be about two months until that became official with the Medicare program, we were able to get paid for patients, whom we saw after April 2. Years later, Carolyn did a return survey to our twenty-seven thousand-square-foot offices, and she and I reminisced about the first survey and the impression it had on both of us. It's funny how some dates and particulars you never forget. I don't think I'll ever forget April 2, 1985, and our Medicare number, 23–7172.

At this time, I was still performing multiple roles in the company—marketer, janitor, clerk, nurse, on-call scheduler, and nurse aide if needed. My husband remembers that time as being one of which we never could sit through a movie or dinner without being paged. I worked from morning until I dropped over at night. It was an exciting and highly energized time—all the work was a labor of love.

From the day I started the company, the first of November, 1984, I never doubted that I would succeed. I would not allow thoughts of doubt to enter my mind. You cannot succeed if you doubt yourself. However, especially that first year, plenty of people outside of my family doubted that I would be successful. I remember a nurse who came to interview, and she looked at me during the interview and asked me if we were a "fly-by-night agency." I told her that no, we weren't, but despite all I said, I knew she didn't believe me. As she left the interview, I knew she wouldn't take the job, and indeed, she didn't. For a moment, as she walked out, a thought of discouragement entered my mind, but I distinctly remember the moment and how I pushed that thought out of my head. In the world you're creating, failure is not an option to be considered. You must always believe that you'll succeed even if the thought appears irrational.

I received the name of an attorney from my insurance person. He helped me with everything I needed to get organized correctly and legally, which was especially helpful, since I had no knowledge of what needed to be done. He gave me the name of an accountant that he recommended. The attorney was very helpful and remained a friend for years; however, the relationship with the accountant ran into problems almost immediately. I met with him in his office, which was billowing with cigarette smoke. He chain smoked through our entire meeting. As I described my operations to him, he worked his calculator. He looked up at me, through the smoke, with his cigarette dangling from his mouth, and quite cynically told me that he didn't see how my business could possibly work out. I congenially got out of there as quickly as I could and later let him know that I wouldn't require his services. I could not allow anyone to be a part of my business who did not believe in me and what I was doing. There are plenty of people who won't believe in you; don't subject yourselves to them. Surround yourself with people who believe in you and avoid people who don't. This isn't the same as surrounding yourself with yes men. A yes man or yes woman, as the case may be, is someone who tells you what you want to hear no matter what they really think. You don't want that because while it may stroke your ego for a while, in the long run it will be damaging to the organization. You want people around you who tell you the truth, give their honest opinions, *and* believe in you.

Two other incidents of discouragement in the early months of that first business are very memorable to me. Shortly after I was up and running, I made an appointment with a local durable medical supply company's owners. They were located just two blocks from me. I walked to the appointment, and once in front of them, gave them my best business presentation. The two of them looked at me, and the only thing they said was, "How old are you?" I could see immediately that as a young woman I was not being taken seriously. I walked the two blocks back to my office. I was discouraged for the first block. Then I held my head up, brushed them out of my mind, and got back to the work of building my company. I didn't receive any referrals from them, as I suspected I wouldn't after that meeting. However, a few years later, when I was successful, it was those men who called and asked for a meeting with me. You see, people might belittle you and not treat you with respect when you start, but when you become successful, the age and gender issues disappear, at least on the surface. Success in the world you create is an equalizer.

The second memory has to do with bankers. I knew that I needed more capital in order to make payroll and fund our growth, so I decided to apply to the Small Business Administration for a loan.

I filled out the application and went to meet with two bankers from a large bank located in downtown Detroit who worked with the government, funding SBA loans. This meeting was very similar to the one with the durable medical equipment owners. It didn't take long for them to tell me that they couldn't offer me a loan. As I left the bank and walked to my car, I felt as if I could hear them laughing as I walked out. I drove a short distance with a heavy heart. Then I pushed those bankers out of my mind; I would find a way to do it without them! I would not let them stop me. With or without those bankers, I would succeed! I learned that day what I've still found to be true; banks only really want to lend money to people who don't need it.

I remained focused on growing the company with the clear purpose and vision that I had formed in my mind and communicated to my staff. From the very first day, I defined my world the way I wanted it to be and not by the competition. I didn't even give much thought to competition. I was cognizant of the competition enough to know who they were and what they offered, but I didn't spend much time thinking about them. I believed myself to be on a different plane in a way, and I just concentrated on my own vision.

That first year it was difficult to get potential referral sources to change their referral patterns and give us a chance. But I stayed in front of those people, and eventually a competitor would stumble, and I'd get my foot in the door. Once I was given a chance, people could see that we were special, that we lived up to our advertising, and had integrity and delivered quality care. As I became more successful and started speeding past the competition, I didn't bother to look back to see what they were doing. Looking back only slows your progress and makes it easier to stumble. Keep your eyes forward and focused.

Find a hook for your company. Find something that makes you different from all the others. For my first company, it was being a one-stop shop. For my current company, I've developed a niche. Whatever you decide to do, define your world, make your vision clear, write your formula for success, and then stick to it. What do I mean by formula for success? Your formula is a list of those ingredients that will create that world for you and make your business successful. For instance, for

Personal Home Care it was caring for every patient as if they were our grandmother, hiring every staff person as if they were going to care for our grandmother, and making a positive difference in the life of each person we touched every day. You may be wondering why I don't have financial goals and indicators as a part of that formula. Here's why: having income greater than expenses (profit) and positive cash flow is absolutely necessary to run a company that will succeed. Let's just call those "givens." Having that formula for what makes you special and defines your world is what makes the difference between just being another company out there and being that very special company that will change not only your world, but the world of everyone with whom you come into contact.

Chapter Four: Creating the Environment

Creating the environment of the company is a very important step in building your own world. The physical space is one part of that environment you create. The culture of the company is the other. In the case of my company, the physical environment was created mostly for the employees because customers in the home care business rarely visit the company offices. In your situation, you may be designing the physical space for the client/customer and the staff. My theory is that it really doesn't matter whether you're designing your space for just employees or for customers and employees because we want to treat both our clients and employees as customers. The culture of the company, that is how it feels to work in the company, in a large way will create the perception and reality of this world of yours. You make the environment one that you want—one that reflects you. My style may be much different than yours; however, I will describe the environment I created for myself as a model for you.

First of all, the physical environment is one that, from the beginning, I created to be professional yet beautiful. Even in those first days, I chose new and quality furnishings. Looking the part of what you want to portray will assist you in turning the look into reality. We spend the better part of our day at work, so shouldn't we be surrounded by things that make us feel good? And if you really appreciate your staff, shouldn't they be surrounded by a nice environment as well? When I visit offices in which the furniture is ugly and in bad repair, I imagine how those employees must feel that they are not appreciated. I doubt that they are, because nice, used furniture can be purchased at very reasonable prices if new furniture is too expensive. Creating a nice environment for staff is not hard to do.

My offices were professional yet warm. Clean is important, and having policies regarding how even your desks should look, whether or not you want people eating at their desks, and whether they can bring items from home for their office, are important issues to clarify. My belief is that people should not eat at their desks, excepting a small snack. When visiting other businesses, I have encountered people eating at their desks, and every time I have found the situation unpleasant, unappealing, and unprofessional. In addition, people need to get away from their desks once in awhile for a break—especially lunch. It will increase their productivity in the long run to take time for a breather and to become refreshed.

I have attended seminars at the Disney Institute in which we were given access to behind the scenes at Disney World. As terrific as Disney is at customer service and human resources, I was amazed to find that little care was taken behind the scenes to make the environment appealing for staff. Once you leave the perfect "stage" created for the customers at Disney World, you find the employees' area a bit drab with little effort at making it aesthetic for them. In the business world and especially in the healthcare business world, employees are as important a customer as the consumers themselves because if you don't have great employees, your consumers will not be well cared for or happy. So, I believe that the behind-the-scenes environment should be as lovely as you would have it for a customer. When the company reached the size that we needed a large building of our own, we carefully designed and decorated the entire building to be calm and aesthetically pleasing for the staff. Even the stairwells were wallpapered and kept in beautiful condition. Since the employees mostly used the stairs, I thought that it was important that it be decorated as well. In the healthcare industry, while men remain substantially in the executive positions, women workers dominate the industry. Many of my employees were single mothers, trying to raise families. In my new building, I dedicated the artwork to mothers and children. Throughout the building were pictures, beautifully framed, depicting the relationship between mother and child.

The second part of creating the environment you want for your company is creating the culture. How does it feel to work in your company? Once again the consideration is that we spend the best part of our day at work. I want to feel good at work, and I want my employees to feel good as well. Employees who feel good about themselves and the company while at work are more productive. So think about and define how you want it to feel at your company. I would suggest that you start by being sincere about the environment you are creating and sincere about treating your staff well. Many executives and business owners miss the most obvious and important ingredient to having an environment that is productive and that is that they need to be truly nice and caring to people. When I attended the human resource course at Disney, during one of the discussions, the facilitator asked the group the question can sincerity be faked? A woman immediately answered, yes, absolutely! But my response to that is to disagree. People can sense fake, and they don't like it.

Another component to creating your culture is deciding how you're going to treat family-related issues. The biggest difference between my healthcare organization and the typical healthcare organization was that a woman sat in the top executive chair. Although I was not a single mom myself, I was sensitive to the issues of the employee and their families, especially the single parents. We were careful to consider the needs of the family and tried to be flexible with employees taking calls from home and having to deal with family concerns. When national Take Your Daughters to Work Day came into being, we jumped on the band wagon in a big way, keeping true to the reason for it. The day was started because studies showed that daughters were socialized into less assertive roles than boys and then achieved less. Creating an exciting day for them to learn about occupations and have a chance to work with their mothers and fathers was a counter to that problem. We also created a separate Take Your Sons to Work Day so that boys could also enjoy the day at work with Mom and Dad, and, yet, we could stay true to the purpose of Daughters Day. We found an extra advantage that came from this program and others like it in which family gets involved at work. When we needed employees to work extra with longer hours, the family was much more supportive because they had a relationship with our workplace too and a better understanding of what their parent did at work.

Another part of the culture of the workplace has to do with how the employee is expected to look and to act. We were clear about dress code and conduct. A professional look was required, and discourteousness did not have a place in our environment. I found that if someone made it through the interview process and was later found to be a disagreeable and discourteous person, they eventually did not feel comfortable and would leave the organization. Over the years I received numerous remarks on the friendliness and niceness of our staff. These remarks came from customers, visitors, potential employees, and auditors. It was an expected part of our culture, and so it became reality. In later years when it became popular to have a casual day, we succumbed to the pressure and requests against my better judgment. Now as I start a new company, I do not have the casual-dress policy because I found that people act the part they are dressed. Casual became too casual, and then sloppy, and behavior followed the dress. For me, it just didn't work; for you and your world, it might be just what you're looking for. Remember as you read this book it's about creating what you are and like and want that makes it your world.

The president of the company sets the tone. Part of setting the tone is to be a champion for your employees. The president's job is to set the culture, set the pace, live the example, and cheer the employees on. I expected people to do great things, and that's exactly what they did. Nitpicking over lunch times and break times is counterproductive to me. Expect people to do a great job, and they will! If they're doing a great job, what do you care what time they take for lunch? It doesn't matter if they're doing a great job, right? Once, when my children were fairly young, a woman who knew me outside of work asked me what my secret was for having such well-behaved and nice kids. The question caught me off guard, and I don't think I even gave her an answer. But later, in retrospect, I realized that my children behaved because I expected them to behave. It's the same in the workplace. The employees, the talented people on your team, will do what you expect them to do, whatever that expectation is.

Of course, as the president of the company, an important component to creating a great environment is to make your attitude and behavior consistent on a day-to-day basis. No matter what's happening at home, what's happening on the board of directors, or what problems there may be with the business, the tone you walk into the office with will set the entire tone for the company. So even if you're having a difficult day, you must walk among the staff with a smile and friendly hello. Ask them how their day is going, remember their kid's names, make it personal with them—you are the champion of the business, the cheerleader of the team, and in a way the George Washington of the Continental Army. In good times and in bad, your consistency of attitude and leadership will drive the entire company. This is something to always be mindful of and never to underestimate.

It is important that you give great care to how you treat people in and out of the organization on a daily basis. I became more aware of how important this was as I gained more exposure in the media and as my company grew larger. You will be growing a reputation for yourself from that first moment you start business, and your reputation will become your greatest asset or detriment, depending on how you treat people and whether or not you act with integrity.

Your ultimate goal in creating your environment is to create one that people will flock to. Whether it's great customers or talented people, you want to attract both in great numbers! You want to make employees and customers feel good about you, and that means you just plain want to make them feel good! So start creating that environment that reflects the best of you, reflects your vision, and is worthy of this great world of yours!

Chapter Five: Building a Team of Superstars

When I was interviewed by Detroit Crain's after being named one of Crain's 40 Under 40, the interviewer asked me what my greatest leadership accomplishment had been so far. I really didn't even have to hesitate. My answer was building a team of superstar staff. I had fantastic people all throughout the company—truly a team of superstars. However, when I started the company, I wasn't able to attract the people with the fabulous resumes because my company was new, and I was young, and the known talented people just weren't interested. But what I did attract were nurses desperate to get off the night shift, caregivers that had cared for a loved one but had no official experience, and clerical staff who had spent the last ten to fifteen years raising their children with little workplace experience. From those hires I built one of, if not the most, talented team in the industry.

One great thing about starting a company from scratch, is that you don't inherit a lot of bad hires or employees you wish you didn't have. I was fortunate to be able to carefully hire one person at a time, building a team that was extraordinary, and you can do the same thing. I have found the following secrets to building that superstar team.

1. *Hiring with care is essential and cannot be overemphasized.* While an interviewee may not have the resume that reflects the experience you'd like to see, what you really want to look for is an applicant's people skills and work ethic. The questions you ask them should try to draw out whether or not they have those two things. Two of my favorite interview questions are what can you bring

to this job that no one else interviewing can bring? And what does your perfect job look like? How they answer these questions will tell you a lot about what they think of themselves and the ideal place where they'd like to be. Another great technique is to ask them to tell you about themselves. You will glean information about the person that you could never have asked from a human resource legal perspective. It's amazing what people will tell you. I remember one girl who, after being asked this question, told me a story about her life and boyfriend and the fact that she kept a handgun in her truck—enough to know really that she was going to be a risky hire.

Checking references verbally is very advantageous, as people will often tell you things about the potential employee that they would never put in writing for fear of being sued. Also, it is good to verify written recommendations for authenticity. I once had a young man interview for a live-in position, and he came with a written recommendation from a priest. When I called the priest to authenticate the recommendation, it was determined that he had stolen the stationary and written the reference himself, and he had been suspected of elder abuse in the past.

During the interview and hiring process and later when offering a position, it is important that your expectations are made very clear. You want to make clear not only the job requirements but also what policies are especially important. They should clearly know the mission of the company as well and your vision for the company.

You design a company to reflect you and your values; this is your prerogative as the business owner and something to take not only seriously but not to be ashamed of. I learned that from the Disney organization. Disney has very specific standards of appearance and behavior. These aren't negotiable standards. For instance, men are not allowed to have facial hair unless it's a part of the role they are playing. You can have non-negotiable standards too—just be very specific about these standards from the interview process and going forward, and then be consistent with your standards. Sometimes, people will try to wear you down to change or lessen your standards; don't give in! Those standards are probably just as important now as the day you wrote them. I have distinct standards in regard to dress, hygiene, behavior, and corporate culture. I spell it out during the interview and then again at orientation. They are given a handbook so that they can refer back to the standards later if necessary. I let them know that if they can't embrace the policies regarding dress and appearance, use of profanity, and various other policies that are important to me and the mission of the company, then it would be best that they find employment in a place where they would be a better fit. This is very important toward the successful completion of creating this world for yourself. These policies need to fit you, your values, and how you want working at your company to feel.

2. *Keep your mission always before your employees.* Starting with the interview and then on a continual basis throughout the organization, there should be no question as to what the mission of your organization is. You must keep visual reminders where people can be reminded every day whether it's a little sign in the elevator, a notation on the pay stubs, or a reminder on their name tags, the mission should be frequently and easily seen. These visual reminders are good and useful but only as effective as the message that is actively lived among the management staff, starting with you! At Personal Home Care, our mission was to make a difference in each life we touched *because people feel better at home.* At Celebration Home Care, it is to give uncompromised quality care to every individual every time *because every day at home is a celebration.* Again, the Disney organization is great at keeping their mission ever before their staff. To augment the mission, it's great to have parties and recognition that springboard off of your mission statement. For instance, we

had a recognition program where staff or clients could nominate a staff member for the caught-in-the-act award. They were caught in the act of making a difference or giving uncompromised quality care. Each nomination was put into a monthly drawing for prizes, and their nominations and testimonials were then published in the monthly newsletter. The idea of keeping the mission ever before them ties directly into my next point, which is:

3. *Give your staff something greater than themselves to work for.* Getting up every day to go to a job that just fills the time and delivers a paycheck is really a miserable existence. People want something great—at least something greater than themselves as a reason to go to work, a reason to get up in the morning. Now, in my business, the healthcare business and particularly the home healthcare business, taking care of people who are sick in the place they love more than anywhere and making a difference in their lives, giving uncompromised qual-

ity care, is a really easy sell as something greater than the individual. It's an ethical, moral, and spiritual calling! But even if you're in the business of making widgets, you can make the mission bigger than the individual. Let me take this just a little further; it's never about money, or profit—though it may very well be about prestige and being the very best. People don't want to get up every day and go to work just for a salary even if it's a big fat salary. If they are doing that, then they are nothing more than hamsters on a tread wheel. People want to get paid a fair wage, but more importantly, they want to do something that is *important,* and even more than that they want to *feel* important. Those of you who are *Cheers* fans, think back to the episode where one of the staff was going in to meet with management to demand a raise. They came out with no raise but an important title and were thrilled! People, or at the least the people you want in *your* organization, are not doing the job simply for the money but to be important or do something important. But that also means at the same time that they should never be taken advantage of and be given a low salary either. Fair pay for a job well done is something important, while they do something that is bigger than they are. This makes an industrious, honest employee shine!

4. *Celebrate everything large and small!* Early on, I started to celebrate every accomplishment large and small even during those years when we didn't have a lot of money. It doesn't take much to bring in pizza and maybe a bottle of fake champagne to celebrate an achievement, and it's so much fun to take time out of the day to rejoice in our accomplishments. Find an excuse to celebrate frequently. This isn't time wasted because staff will feel good about themselves and working with you, and their attitude and productivity will only increase. I found celebration so essential to success that I named my most recent company Celebration Home Care. It doesn't have to be much, but when your company has even

small successes, do something to celebrate, and as you get bigger and more successful, your celebrations will get bigger too, but never forget the little every day celebrations.

5. *Thank someone for something every day, and every day show your appreciation.* As we discussed earlier, it's important to expect the best from your staff. And after you expect the best and they give it, your staff needs to know that you're grateful. Recognition is important. It's done with employee-of-the-month programs but it must go beyond that. Thank someone for something every day. When you recognize their work, call them by name, remember their families in your conversations with them, and you will endear yourself to them, and they want to work all the harder to accomplish your mission and vision.

   The first nurse I hired came to me because she was a single mom with young kids, and she wanted to get off the night shift. Peggy was willing to take a chance on an unknown company to get on the day shift. She was one of the best people I ever hired and was influential within the company and to our success. We laughed many times over the years, remembering her first day on the job because I asked her what I had told her I'd pay her because I couldn't remember! One day when I was out making marketing calls, I swung through McDonald's for lunch. As I drove through the drive-through area, I looked in the rearview mirror and saw Peggy in the car behind me. I smiled and waved, and then when I got to the window to pay, I thought, *how fun it would be to pay for her lunch too*, so I paid for both our orders and then went on my way, not thinking another thing about it. Later that day when I was back at the office, Peggy came in and gave me a great big hug and said something I'll never forget: "No one's ever done anything like that for me before." What had I done? Spent one dollar and seventy-five cents on her lunch? It hit me that such a small gesture could bring such a positive response. From then on, I tried to remember and do the little things as often as possible. In the following months we struggled with cash flow problems, and somehow she found out. Peggy called me and offered me the money in her savings account so that I could make payroll. That fifteen hundred dollars was a lot of money to her and to me. You see, it never fails; when you appreciate others, you eventually receive much back in return. I received even more through the years, as Peggy grew with the company and eventually became our Chief Operating Officer.

6. *Work on deficiencies as they occur.* If people for whatever reason aren't working out, do them and you a favor, and work with them early on to correct whatever deficiencies they have. I err on the side of giving that person extra effort. When it's time for an evaluation or when you know it's not going to work out, the employee should already know why because you've worked on the issue. If it isn't working out for whatever reason, whether they don't have the skills to do the job, or whether they aren't making the effort to do what is needed, it is very important that you either redirect them

to a job that is within their skill set or let them know that it isn't working out at your company. For instance, sometimes we promote great line workers to management, and it just doesn't end up being their forte. In these instances, though it may be a little hard on the ego for the manager, offering them a position similar to what they did before they were promoted can save a good employee and also send the message that we don't penalize people who try something new and bigger if it doesn't work out.

On those occasions when there is no alternative but to separate the employee from the company, I try to always treat the employee as I would like to be treated. That day many years ago when I was fired and walked to my car by security with all the shame and humiliation that I felt is forever imprinted on my mind. As a result, I give all the dignity possible to any person I am letting go from the company. There are times, of course, when circumstances are such that extra security measures are required, but I find those to be rare.

7. *Give opportunities to grow and help employees be the best they can be.* Over the years I have learned that my greatest joy and, perhaps, my greatest talent is helping people become the best they can be. The success stories are many. In my early days, I hired a girl to work part time doing pre-billing work in the evening. She was about to be divorced and had a young son. One evening when Diane was working and I was there working late, she came into my office and asked me what future she had in my company because she could make more money being on welfare than she was earning from me, but she wanted to work. I told her that there were no limits to what she could accomplish at the company if she worked hard. She went on to develop as a great biller then managed the billing department. Always wanting to try new things and progress, in the twenty years she worked with me, she also handled our managed care contracts and became a top sales person. She remains today very successful at all she endeavors, capable of doing anything she wishes to do. In one of

the last conversations I had with her as I left my company, she told me that she would be always grateful for the chance I gave her over twenty years earlier. I gave Diane the opportunity, and I believed in her—she did the rest.

You see, there are a lot of philosophical arguments about whether or not you can motivate people. Some say only the individual can motivate him or herself. I believe that you can provide opportunities for people, and you can believe in them and give them the tools to succeed. So many times I have believed in women who didn't believe in themselves. Whether it was bad employment experiences, growing up in a rough, uncaring home, or coming out of a bad marriage, so many women that I've come in contact with during my years of being in business have not been appreciated or believed in before coming to my company. How simple and easy it is to do those two things—appreciate a person and believe in them—and then how much enjoyment it is to watch them thrive and grow in the environment you create. Not too long ago I interviewed a woman who apologized for not having worked in the last fifteen years as she raised her family. I told her not to underestimate herself; the skills necessary to manage a family were the same skills I was looking for in being a receptionist for my office. She has turned out to be a great employee. What I have accomplished in hiring her is bringing a new employee back into the workplace that will not only do a great job for me, but will also have an added level of loyalty because I gave her a chance. It's fun to do and especially fun to watch. What a thrill!

Along the way, ask employees, even randomly when managing by walking around, what you can do for them to support them, make their job easier, better. Always ask at evaluation time. Don't worry; the answers will not be self serving. Your staff knows ways to make the job better, easier, more efficient, and if they feel empowered and like you are listening, they'll fill you in too. They must feel that change is possible,

> so you will have to follow-up and follow through with what you learn from staff.
>
> Give people opportunities to grow within the company and try new things. Think of each employee as a diamond in the rough that will shine when given a chance—you will have a wellspring of talent coming right out of your own organization. Sometimes they have to leave your employ to grow, but many times when people left, they later came back to me with richer experiences to give to our company.

I knew early on that my formula for building a staff of superstars was very good, but it wasn't until the end of my time with Personal Home Care that I found out just how good my formula was. When it was made clear that my company was being merged into a larger company, top staff started leaving immediately, fearful of losing their jobs. In fact the first person left the very day the merger was announced. From the time the merger of our parent company was announced until the time that I actually left the company was a little over one year. Keeping the organization going during that time was perhaps the most difficult thing I've ever had to accomplish. It was during that time when we were kept in the dark about what was purposed with our company that I wondered even if the company could survive. What started to happen and continued to happen for the next fifteen months was amazing to me. As people left, other people equally or more talented than the person who left would step up and do a great job. This happened time after time. I found out that superstars were throughout the company, just waiting for opportunity to shine, and as a result, we continued on until my departure, maintaining operations when a company with less talented staff would have crumbled. I saw in the purest form that these secrets, this formula for success, absolutely works and works even in the long run and under pressure.

Chapter Six: Customer Service and Quality

On the day that I started Personal Home Care, in addition to the fabulous advice my dad gave me regarding my accountant and attorney, was the advice he gave me regarding customer service. He said the world is full of companies giving lousy customer service. Give great customer service, he told me, and then I will stand out from the rest of the companies. That business advice was true then and just as true today.

Think back over the last week and all the people with whom you came into contact. Were there any moments of fabulous customer service that you can remember? Chances are that if you did get great customer service, you will remember that incident. And do you know why? Because those incidents in our lives are rare indeed. Just last night I was at an award dinner, and the person at the table next to me, whom I didn't know before that evening, started telling a story of getting fabulous customer service when returning some clothes that his wife had purchased at a department store. He didn't give the name of the store, and so I asked him, "Was that store Nordstrom?" "Why, yes," he said, "it was." He told the story of how his wife asked him to return an entire outfit for her. So he took the dress, shoes, and undergarments necessary for the outfit back to Nordstrom. The first department he visited in what he thought would be an extended journey to several departments to make the necessary returns offered to return all of the items for him. He was amazed and pleased at the level of customer service. My guess that he was at Nordstrom was easy because of all the stores I've shopped at, including high end, low end, and in between, none have ever delivered that level of service for me. Nordstrom not only delivers but delivers every time that same great customer service that has made them famous. There is another famous brand name—the Ritz Carlton Hotels—that also delivers that wonderful customer service every time, and it just so happened that the event I was attending was at a Ritz Carlton, and I experienced that level of service in a memorable experience. Eight hundred people were attending the award ceremony, and when the evening ended, of course, all eight hundred of us headed for the door and the valet at the same time. So there we stood, en masse, and after about twenty minutes of seeing no procedure for obtaining my car, I left the car area and went back into the Ritz to the coat check desk. There I encountered two staff members. I said to them that I knew it wasn't their area, but did they happen to know what the procedure was to obtain my car? From what I could see, people weren't handing their tickets to anyone, and cars were randomly being brought up for pick-up. The staff person said they didn't know, but one of them would accompany me back out to the valet area and would find out what was going on with my car for me. And accompany me she did! Now, it turned out that the valet stand was located to the left, and due to the large group of people, I didn't see that I was supposed to give the valet person my ticket and he would bring my car up. I did that, and very quickly my car was retrieved, and I left the Ritz Carlton with yet another fabulous experience.

When I started Personal Home Care, I followed my dad's advice, and we became known for our quality and customer service. After I left Personal Home Care, I had a vision for a new company. It would be a company providing private duty home care only, and this company would celebrate each day of the life of each patient and employee. Shortly after leaving Personal and while I was starting to put together this new company, Celebration Home Care, something happened that would change my life and the life of Celebration Home Care forever.

My mother needed to have surgery—nothing too big, a hysterectomy with a little bit of extra work to help repair what got pushed around carrying four of us. Just a standard surgery, no big deal. The day of surgery, I picked Mom up at her condo at five a.m. so we could be at the hospital by six a.m. She was waiting at the door when I pulled up, my beautiful, vibrant mother who didn't look old enough to be my mom. Always healthy and athletic, trim and energetic, always wanting to look fabulous, this morning being no exception, with full makeup, including lipstick and fake nails. When I was in high school some of my friends called her Jackie Kennedy, and that's what she was like—stylish and beautiful. We checked in at the admitting desk, and the nurse came to take her back to pre-op. She walked back with the nurse, turned, and gave me a little wave. The surgery took a lot longer than expected, and my sister and I were concerned, but eventually the surgeon came out and said it went well, and we went back to see her in recovery. When it was time to transfer her to her room after recovery, the nurse told us to go get a cup of coffee and to come back after she was settled in. Thirty minutes later we returned to the room, and when we walked into the room I immediately knew that something was wrong. Two hospital personnel were in the room, and they had Mom sitting straight up in bed, and they were trying to get her to tell them her name and respond to questions. I looked on the clipboard setting on the bedside table and saw that the nurse had written a blood pressure of sixty over forty. After what seemed an eternity but was probably two minutes, I said, “It’s time to call the doctor.” They called a code Emma, which is the equivalent of one level down from a code blue. Healthcare workers streamed into the room, and we went into a vacant room across the hall and prayed. She was taken to intensive care, and after volumes of fluid, her pressure improved, and she regained consciousness. She remained in ICU through the night for observation, and we were relieved, believing this to be an anesthesia reaction.

The next morning, my sister and I were with Mom, who was still in intensive care and it became evident quite quickly that the nurse was irritated to have such a well patient in ICU. Mom had breakfast and was going to get up to the bathroom, so we stepped out to get some lunch. The last thing she said to us is that she wished she could feel well. We were just leaving lunch when we received a frantic call from my brother. He was at the hospital, and he said, “Mom isn’t right.” We soon learned that he walked into her room in ICU and found her sitting in bed, holding her call light button with the bell ringing. Her oxygen was hanging off her face, and she was incoherent. No one answered the light, and he started searching the halls for someone to help. Finally when, in his desperation, he decided he would have to ring the fire alarm, Mom's nurse appeared. When my brother said something was wrong, she rolled her eyes at him. Upon entering the room, she quickly found out that her "well" patient was deteriorating at a very fast rate. Mom was quickly going into a coma. We were to later learn that she had suffered a blood clot to the midbrain, and the next days were spent in prayer as Mom fought for her life. We never left Mom alone in the hospital again—we were afraid to. The next thirty days in the hospital and rehab unit located in the same hospital and the encounters with healthcare workers that we experienced were an eye-opening education on the state of healthcare in the United States today. Mom had several code Emmas called on her while she was in the hospital and rehab because she would quite suddenly stop responding, and her blood pressure would drop to 60/40 and below. One such episode happened during therapy after the therapist told me with apparent distain that she was sleeping during physical therapy and snoring. When I went to the table to talk with her, she was unable to be aroused. Now, not so smug, the therapist raced her back to her room where the code was called. While I sat outside her room and they worked on her, the supervisors stood right by me, looking at vacation pictures. I was petrified, in tears, beyond hope, desperate, and they were looking at vacation pictures. That moment and all it represented burned into my mind.

To most staff she was just the stroke in room 315. She was extremely fatigued, now had a funny squeaky voice, and the iris in her right eye was so deviated to the right that you could barely see it. She couldn't remember anything in the short term and was so weak she could hardly walk. Many couldn't see past this disheveled, sick woman to the beautiful, accomplished person she really was. So one day I brought in a picture of her with her grandchildren at the beach as a reminder that this was the person they were dealing with. She was not just a number, a diagnosis, and a lot of health problems, but a person who deserved care and respect. And what happened to her there, even though it was just one hospital, I have to believe is fairly representative of hospitals as a whole, especially hospitals that are a part of a system located in a metropolitan area. That experience ended up refining my vision for this new company I was starting. It wasn't the incompetence so much, though there was that, but the overall lack of consideration and poor customer service that alarmed me. One night when it was my "shift" to spend the night with Mom, I slept next to her, curled up in a lazy boy chair on the rehab unit. The bright overhead lights suddenly came on, and a male attendant came in with an all-too apparent dislike of the fact that family thought they needed to be there. He was large and rough and made sure he woke us both fully up to take her vital signs. When he was finished with his tasks and just as he flicked out the lights, he said, "Try and get some sleep now."

As I shifted around in the chair again, trying to get comfortable and warm, I thought to myself, *Is this the best we can do? In this great country with the best and most expensive healthcare in the world, is this really the best we can do?* My mom deserved to be treated with respect and consideration. My mom and every other patient deserved uncompromised quality of care every time. I thought right then,

I can do it better, and I will do it better. I will provide private duty home care with Celebration Home Care that will be uncompromised. It will be different and better than other private duty home care company because every patient deserves uncompromised care. That vision is our vision now, and to provide uncompromised care and customer service to every patient every time is what we are in business to do. No exceptions.

When you are providing healthcare, it isn't just about providing a marketing edge for your business. When you provide healthcare, it is your moral and ethical responsibility to provide uncompromised quality care. We are touching human lives! But even outside of healthcare, isn't uncompromised quality still a necessity and a moral obligation? When someone is paying you for a product or service, shouldn't you provide them with the product or service they paid for? Here's a concept to add to that thought—give them *more* in value than they paid for. It's a concept explained in the book *The Science of Getting Rich* by Wallace Wattles. If you and everyone else gave more in value than you were paid, the world would advance and grow to a land of plenty. It is when we give less than we are paid that the world suffers a lack, and that lack compounds. Try this as a little experiment sometime: give more than is expected, leave a place better than you found it, praise someone even more than they deserve. You will in turn find that extra that you gave come back to you.

Here are the important components of an excellent customer service program in your organization.

1. *Make the commitment and declare it your passion to have excellent quality and customer service within your organization.* An organization must have the commitment and dedication for this, start with you if it is to succeed within the entire company.

2. *Live the commitment.* If you give it lip service but don't emphasize, reemphasize, exemplify, and practice commitment, it just won't work. So make it real, have the vision and commitment in front of the staff constantly.

3. *Expect the commitment from every staff member.* Make customer service expectation a

part of every interview, every hire, every job description, and every evaluation. And if a staff member does not live that customer service as expected, it will be apparent to them and others that they are not a fit within the organization. A person not living that expectation for you cannot stay because it will slowly start of deterioration of all you've worked for.

4. *Follow through with the commitment for the long run.* Many organizations make a strong start, but few follow through. Stick with it. Monitor it and make it personal for you. I follow up with customer-service complaints myself; it's a great way to know what really goes on in your organization.

When Farmer Jack first moved into my small town, they had a great grand opening. The floors were sparkling, the bottle return slots clean, and cashiers were standing at the ends of their aisles, inviting you to their aisle. The customer service was fantastic. It wasn't long though before the floors were dirty, the bottle returns full and sticky, and the cashiers grumpy and talking about their breaks. They just couldn't follow through with the customer service. About three years later they were out of business.

The start of Celebration Home Care was delayed with my mom's illness, but she ended up inspiring the intensity and passion of our mission at Celebration and in essence became Celebration's first patient. How appropriate that my first company was started to care for my grandmother and my second to care for my mother. When I'm talking with a customer about caring for a loved one at home, one thing they know for sure is that I know what I'm talking about from experience. They know it is personal for me. Make it personal for you and your business as well. And in this world of lousy customer service, you will differentiate yourself, and that will make all the difference in your world.

Chapter Seven: Becoming a Leader

Thousands of reams have been written about leadership and what it means to be a leader. The need for, purpose of, and phenomenon of leadership has been studied and expounded upon ever since the beginning of the world. According to Stogdill's *Handbook of Leadership*, leadership is a universal human phenomenon. Regardless of culture, leadership occurs universally among peoples. J.M. Burns said, "Leadership is one of the most observed and least understood phenomena on earth." Our society today longs for great leaders.

You may have the gift of leading people. You may already, without any education or mentoring, exhibit extraordinary leadership skills. However, if you do not, please don't lose heart. While I do not believe that absolutely anyone can become a great leader, I do believe that leadership skills in many ways can be learned. There are important components of leadership that we will discuss in this chapter, parts of which can never be ignored if you want to become a great leader.

We will keep our definition of leadership simple and use the definition of leadership as given by Stephen P. Robbins: "Leadership is the ability to influence a group toward the achievement of goals."

It's important to make a difference between leadership and management because they are absolutely not the same thing. Leadership is about creating a vision, communicating the vision, and inspiring others toward bringing the vision to reality. Management is concerned with implementing the vision and strategy and handling the day-to-day operations.

There is an emotionally charged romantic idea of leadership that in many instances is real. It is this romantic, emotional idea of leadership that has enabled men and women to lead people and companies forward and to accomplish great ideals, great causes, and accomplish great or horrible things. The emotional search for the great leader is what charges our national elections to a large degree. We *want so badly* to be lead by great leaders. But beyond this emotionally charged romantic ideal is the necessity for leaders to have skills in leading. It is when leaders don't have the skills necessary to be great leaders that their attempts fail and become futile no matter how great and charismatic the leader may be. Of course, sometimes behind the charismatic leader who does not have leadership core competencies there are brilliant and talented people who carry the charismatic leader so that sound leadership is carried out even when the leader is weak in the core competencies. However, in time, if the charismatic leader doesn't recognize that this talent is the foundation behind the charisma, then they will most likely depend upon their own wisdom instead of the wisdom of those around him or her and cause an undoing of the leadership success already created.

The core competencies I suggest as vital and necessary to be a great leader I borrow from the curriculum established at Andrews University in their leadership program, of which I was a graduate. They are:

1. Be an effective teacher and mentor with skills in learning strategies, group processes, and mentoring.

2. Be a dynamic change agent with skills in planning and implementing change and developing human resources and public relations.

3. Be an effective organizer with skills in organizational development, managing resources, and interpreting laws, regulations, and policies.

4. Be a collaborative consultant with skills in effective communication, evaluating, assessing, problem solving, and decision making.

5. Be a competent scholar with a working knowledge of ethics and personal and professional development.

6. Have a sound working knowledge of the foundations of leadership.

7. Have a sound working knowledge of theories of leadership and management.

8. Have a sound working knowledge of social systems, family dynamics, community structures, and global development.

9. Have a sound working knowledge of technology and its application.

And especially important when working within the academic field or when implementing change and ideas based on proven research:

10. Be a reflective researcher.

It would stand to reason then, that to increase your leadership abilities, you should increase your competency in these areas. Competencies in any area can be increased through study, experience and mentoring. A leader must have developed core competencies to be an effective leader and then utilize a leadership style as a vehicle for effectively communicating and implementing strategies to make the organization great, for when a leader has developed strong core competencies and has mastered the art of leadership style, a truly great leader emerges. There has been much written and discussed about leadership style. At one time leadership style was pigeonholed into categories that were quite broad. Very popular was the idea of an autocratic leadership style versus a democratic style. Leadership style has also been discussed in terms of traits that a successful leader might exhibit. While researchers haven't been very successful in identifying traits in leaders that guarantee success, it has, however, been helpful for organizations to be able to choose leaders who exhibit the traits that the organization finds works best in the culture of the organization. For instance, a CEO known for his or her axe-cutting approach to cost reduction and organizational transformation wouldn't fit very well in a company that has a strong no-lay-off policy.

Theories of successful leadership styles have concentrated for the most part on looking at leadership behaviors. Quite often the behaviors are in relation to either people or product and tasks.

These different styles are not completely distinct from each other, and you will see that some leadership styles have overlapping boundaries. We will briefly look at the top styles, and we will amalgamate them all together with this idea: the most effective leader is the leader who chooses the most appropriate style for the situation. This is the concept of situational leadership style that has been around for fifty years and that I present here with my own personal twist on the theory.

Directive leadership defines the tasks and roles of the people within the organization and expects people to carry out directions. People are not usually required to know or understand why, and they are not expected to contribute original ideas. Communication is largely one-way. An example of when this style might be used is in time of crisis when the leader must take the responsibility and make needed course corrections. In this situation the decisions needed might be so important, time constraints so tight, and situations so stressful that input by staff would be ineffectual. While this isn't the optimal style on an ongoing basis, directive leadership style definitely has its place.

Supportive leadership focuses on people and relationships and passes on day-to-day decisions, task allocation, and processes to the people within the organization. This leader facilitates and takes part in decisions but allows control to pass to the people. This style is best used when tasks are structured, and, given a well-run organization, this style can bring with it a large amount of employee satisfaction.

Bureaucratic leadership seeks neither attainment of any real results or relationships and may make a good effort to look busy with actual contribution being limited. Organizations create these leaders through strict adherence to procedure as the dominant ethic and risk taking is severely penalized. I do not recommend this leadership style at any time, as it is uncreative and ineffective.

Collaborative leadership seeks ideas and suggestions from the people within the organization though decisions remain the leader's prerogative. The involvement of others in the planning process is considered essential, and the environment is one in which there are feelings of ownership and commitment to organizational goals. This style can be very successful on an ongoing basis, especially when the leader leaves a lot of the decision making power to others.

The charismatic leader uses vision and a willingness to take risks to achieve their vision, along with sensitivity to follower needs to influence followers. Charismatic leaders articulate an appealing vision, provide a sense of continuity for followers by linking the present to a better future, communicating high performance expectations, and expressing confidence that followers can obtain the expectations. They usually do all of this with emotion. The charismatic leader exhibits unconventional behavior and demonstrates courage and conviction about the vision. People working for charismatic leaders are often motivated to work with extra effort and express greater satisfaction. Examples of charismatic leaders include John F. Kennedy, Lee Iacocca, Martin Luther King, and Mary Kay Ash. Sometimes charismatic leaders are born out of extraordinary times, such as F.D. Roosevelt during the Great Depression or Lee Iacocca during the financial difficulties of Chrysler. Charismatic leadership may also have a dark side when the leader uses his or her power to serve their own personal purposes over the needs of the individuals and the organization. Examples of this are Adolf Hitler and Jim Jones.

Transformational leadership inspires followers to transcend their own personal self-interests for the good of the organization. While this style is related to the charismatic style, it goes beyond charismatic leadership because the successful transformational leader instills in followers the ability to question established views and even those established by the leader. The transformational leader takes the vision, believes in it, and never stops constantly selling the vision. They have a lot of energy and commitment, and while seeking to overtly transform the organization, they make an implied promise to followers that they will be transformed in some way as well. They also provide a lot of intellectual stimulation, promoting rational and careful problem solving. This style when used within organizations correlates with low staff-turnover rates, high staff satisfaction, and high productivity, and isn't that what we'd all love to have in our companies?

Visionary leadership is another leadership style related to the charismatic leadership style. It goes beyond charisma and is wrapped around the leader's ability to create and articulate a realistic, credible, attractive vision of the future for an organization or organizational unit, which grows out of and improves upon the present. They have three main qualities: the ability to explain the vision to others, the ability to express the vision not just verbally but through the leader's behavior, and the ability to extend the vision to different leadership contexts. Mary Kay Ash was a visionary charismatic leader while Ronald Regan was one of the greatest visionary leaders. This style is very useful and effective when there's a great change needed in an organization. The leader uses their charisma to energize and move employees toward a new vision and direction for the organization.

You can see now that certain styles are best used in certain circumstances. You may generally have a collaborative leadership style but in time of crisis temporarily switch to a directive style. You may be a transformational leader but when the market changes drastically and the organization needs a drastic change in direction become a visionary leader. As the leader, you make the decision when a style change is necessary based upon your analysis and perception. What's really fun is knowing that leadership style, for most individuals, can be acquired.

Having the right style for the right circumstance is essential to the life of the organization, but no matter what style you have or are using, there are even more important principles of leadership that you must follow in order to be a truly great leader.

> *You must do the right thing because it is right.* I hope your first response is to think, *Well, of course!* Unfortunately it is common today for corporations and leaders within corporations, when faced with the decision of whether to do what is right or to do what is easy and what will create more gain, to do what's easiest and what will produce the most gain at the expense of doing what is right. You must resist the attraction to follow this group no matter the circumstance. I'll give you an example: in the 1990s when my infusion therapy business was getting started, there were some product lines that had very high profit margins. It was commonplace that the big competitors were

paying doctors for their referrals. I couldn't get any of the really great business because of this practice, and I wouldn't agree to the practice, as it was considered fraudulent. I remember one day receiving a call on my cell phone from a local physician. He told me that he had sent us an antibiotic patient, and where was his three hundred fifty dollars? I told him that we didn't pay for referrals, but we would take excellent care of his patient. He said that if he didn't get the money, he wouldn't be referring any additional patients to us, and indeed he didn't. Let me tell you, it was tough keeping the business going when I was one of the few not paying physicians for referrals. In time, however, a major company was indicted for the practice, and the competitors for the most part stopped this activity, and then the playing field evened out. In the meanwhile I didn't have any sleepless nights worrying that federal agents might be knocking at my door.

Practice integrity in your personal and professional your life, and the reputation you will gain will be more valuable than anything else you might acquire. Base your decisions on integrity, and do all things you do just because it is the right thing to do, and the trust you gain from your customers and your staff will be worth anything else you might lose along the way while you were keeping your integrity intact. Still today, years after leaving my first business, I find that my reputation for integrity is strong and well known in the home care industry. I wouldn't trade that for anything.

A great leader will be a servant leader. When I was in my leadership doctoral program and we were studying servant leadership, I remember one particular student who couldn't fathom the idea that she would or should be a servant while being in a leadership position. It seems to many that you can't be a servant and have power. However, many powerful writers have described the importance of servant leadership. Max Depree in his book *Leadership is an Art* puts it this way: "The first responsibility of a leader is to define reality. The last is to say thank you.

In between the two, the leader must become a servant and a debtor." Robert Greenleaf writes in his book *Servant Leadership* when talking about followers that "they will freely respond only to individuals who are chosen as leaders because they are proven and trusted as servants." And then, of course, there is the way Jesus sums it up when he says, "And whoever desires to be first among you, let him be your slave."

It seems to be a part of western culture to want to wield power over another human being. One day when discussing a certain situation with one of my leaders, she remarked that she was in a power struggle with one of the male managers who reported to her. I reminded her that there was no struggle because she was already in the position of power and held all of the power in that situation; therefore, there was no need for a struggle. I have found personally that to try to use power over another person only provokes resistance, while positioning yourself to serve that person drops that resistance and in reality draws that person and their support toward you. For that reason, I like to ask people in many situations and, especially when talking with customers or employees during performance review situations, "What can I do for you?" Say it and mean it, and you will see what a powerful tool it is for you as a leader and as a person.

What often distinguishes a great leader from one that is mediocre or even poor is the ability that leader has to make decisions. The decisions of top leaders are usually the vital decisions of the organization. It seems that as leaders we make decisions that exist somewhere on the continuum of importance all day long. Because decision making is so important, we will take a good look at how we can make the best decisions.

A moral decision is any decision that affects the life of another human being. By that definition, you can see that almost every decision you make as the leader of an organization is a moral one. Keeping that in mind, the importance of each decision and the impact it will have on staff and their families can be sobering. I define for you three types of decision making. We will look at each type and the impact it has on you as a leader.

The first type of decision making and the one taught in business schools and most accepted is rational decision making. In his textbook on organizational behavior, Stephen Robbins states that "the optimizing decision maker is rational." He lists a six-step rational decision-making model:

1. Define the problem.
2. Identify the decision criteria.
3. Allocate weights to the criteria.
4. Develop the alternatives.
5. Evaluate the alternatives.
6. Select the best alternative.

For a lot of the problems we encounter as well as the types of situations that need a decision, rational decision making is a very good way to make that decision. But, as Peter Drucker put it in his article on the effective decision in the Harvard Business

Review, "every decision is a risk-taking judgment." Sometimes rational decision making isn't as cut and dry as the directions for rational decision making would require. That is when the second kind of decision, "intuitive" or non-rational decision making, comes in. Until fairly recently the idea that executives used their intuition, that is, knowledge gained without rational thought, to make effective decisions was not recognized as a legitimate or accepted concept for decision making (Rowan 1986). However, the research of Weston H. Agor in the 1980s produced evidence that leaders and managers are making plenty of intuitive decisions and are most likely to make intuitive decisions under the following circumstances:

- When there is little precedent to draw on.
- When variables are less scientifically predictable.
- When "facts" are limited.
- When facts do not clearly point the way to go.
- When analytical data is of little use.

- When there are several plausible alternative solutions from which to choose, with good arguments for each.
- When time is limited, and there is pressure to come up with the right decision, and a high level of uncertainly exits.

Dr. Agor studied over five thousand executives and found some astounding results. His findings showed that intuition is a skill used more often as managers climbed up the management ladder, with the highest amount of intuition used by the top managers (Agor 1984). It was also significant that when these top managers used intuition to make a decision they believed to be correct, they felt a feeling of excitement, almost euphoria, a total sense of commitment, confidence, and enthusiasm for the solution. Conversely, if they sensed an impending decision was an incorrect one, they spoke of feelings of anxiety, discomfort, and sometimes an upset stomach. His research also showed that there was a statistically significant difference in regard to men and women making decisions with intuition. Women consistently scored higher on the intuition scale than men in every group sampled.

Research conducted since that time has shown that fire fighters, jet fighter pilots, and people under fire either in the service or as police officers must make decisions in split seconds when rational decision making would be impossible. The brain literally processes everything that has ever happened to them instantly and helps them decide in a moment of crisis what to do based on all of their experiences from the past. It's really a marvelous demonstration of the intricacy and power of the human brain.

However, since most of our decisions do not fall under the criteria for strictly rational or intuitive decision making, in crisis, we have at our disposal a third option, and that is to use both rational and intuitive skills to make our decisions. In short, we first do all that we can to make a sound rational decision, and then when still faced with an unclear answer use our intuitive skills to make a decision. Frequently, I have known this to happen when faced with a hiring decision in which one or more applicants have similar qualifications and it's difficult to make a decision based on what is on paper alone. At that time you have to go with what's in your gut. You see, the intuitive or right side of your brain can only communicate itself to you with non-verbal cues, such as a gut feeling. Those intuitive decisions are all made on the side of the brain that does not use logic, which is left-brain thinking. Here's the most beautiful part. It has been scientifically proven that the two sides of our brains while operating differently, will work together in unison to make the very best decision. That being known, don't be afraid to use *all* of your decision-making capabilities to generate those decisions so vital to your organization. And don't be afraid to trust those decisions.

I'd like to make one further observation regarding decision making. No matter what type of decision you are making and unless you are in a life-and-death circumstance, you should never make a decision based on fear. Fear is paralyzing, and the emotions of fear will mask the true instincts of your right brain. Some of the mistakes I have made as a leader were made when I was fearful. If I had not taken counsel with my fears, if I had waited to be calmer and had placed more faith in God's ability to help me in time of trouble, I could have averted much pain and turmoil. When you learn how to think properly, there is never a need to make a decision in a fearful state of mind. A great book for learning how to think properly is a book by Wallace Wattles called *The Science of Being Great* and which I've listed in the references and the bibliography on my website.

A leader who is leading a successful organization, especially a leader who is entrepreneurial and doesn't really like to get stuck in the details, will be tempted to move away from operations. It is important that to a certain extent you resist this temptation. You don't want operations to become a quagmire for you, and you certainly don't want to micromanage, but you need to monitor indicators and know enough about operations to be sure your business is running properly and optimally. I suggest having a dashboard of indicators that you review frequently enough to be relevant and to be able to overt a big problem should it be on the rise. On the flip side of that advice, is to never be so close to operations that you can't take time away from everything—absolutely everything—to think, plan, and study. All great leaders take time to do this, with the most recent and notable leader being Bill Gates. It is absolutely the lifeblood of your visionary leadership and what will give you the energy and ideas that will distinguish you from all the rest.

Being a leader at the top of an organization can truly be a very lonely job. Many times you wish you could bounce things off someone else, but you aren't able to do that within the organization. For that reason it will benefit you greatly to start or join a mastermind alliance. A mastermind alliance as defined by Napoleon Hill consists of two or more minds working actively together in perfect harmony toward a common definite objective. Through a mastermind alliance you can appropriate and use the full strength of the experience, training, and knowledge of others just as if they were your own. He also makes these other points: no individual has ever achieved success without the help and cooperation of others and the value of gathering together those of a like mind is self-evident and a group of brains coordinated in a spirit of harmony will provide more thought energy than a single brain, just as a group of electric batteries will provide more energy than a single battery. A mastermind alliance must have a code of ethics that includes confidentiality and must be with people you can trust, and, given that, you can see that the benefits will be immense.

Chapter Eight: The Importance of Mentoring

Have you ever been mentored? For instance, when you had your first job, did anyone take you under their wing and show you the way? Or when you had a baby, did someone help you work through that first week of breastfeeding? I bet you have at least one story of how you've been mentored and how that mentor has influenced you in a mighty way either in your personal or professional life. In my life my father was a strong business mentor, and my mom a strong woman-of-independence mentor. When I was finishing nursing school, I had a head nurse on the hospital unit who helped me gain confidence as a nurse. During my years growing Personal Home Care, my colleagues Joel Pott and Robert Milewski were strong mentors, helping me as I learned how to work within a larger system and with governance issues. Mentors typically play really big roles in our lives.

Gordon F. Shea in his book titled *Mentoring* tells the story of Mentor. Mentor comes from Homer's Odyssey. When Odysseus, King of Ithaca, goes to fight in the Trojan War, he trusts the care of his son, Telemachus, and his household to Mentor, who serves as a trusted teacher and overseer. After the war, Odysseus is condemned to wander for ten years, and Telemachus, now grown, goes in search of his father. Telemachus is accompanied by Athena, goddess of war and patroness of the arts and industry, who assumes the form of Mentor. Eventually father and son are reunited, and together they reclaim the throne and Telemachus's birthright. In time, the word *mentor* became synonymous with trusted advisor, friend, teacher, and wise person.

In a mentoring relationship, one person invests time, energy, and assistance in the growth and development of another person. Historical examples of mentor relationships are Socrates and Plato, Hayden and Beethoven, Freud and Jung, just to name a few. And though our mentors might not be quite so grand, they are, just the same, special people in our lives who help us move toward fulfilling our greatest potential.

There are three types of mentoring relationships, which we will look at here:

- the relationship of senior executive to junior executive
- the relationship of established employee to new employee
- the relationship of adult to young person.

Each of these relationships is quite unique and different from the others, and each is very important in its own way. Let's talk about each type.

The first type of relationship is senior executive to junior executive or, in the case of larger organizations, maybe senior executive to senior executive

with less experience. In my doctoral research on intuitive decision making, I found quite surprisingly, that the executives studied who were highly intuitive, for the most part, had strong mentors who helped them learn how to make good decisions. The importance of mentoring in the successful development of an executive from beginning manager to senior level executive was one of the major findings of my research. And mentoring, while in the past has not been emphasized in the classroom, has started to come into its own importance.

These executive-mentoring relationships can be formal and organized or informal and arise naturally out of the association of one person with another. Whether formal or informal, mentoring supports the individual in many ways. Here is a list of benefits to the person being mentored. The information comes from Harvard business essentials book *Coaching and Mentoring* and was adapted from the work of Kathy E. Kram.

1. The mentor opens doors that would otherwise be closed.

2. The mentor teaches and provides feedback.
3. The mentor supports the protégé and/or acts as a buffer.
4. The mentor encourages new ways of thinking and acting and pushes the protégé to stretch his or her capabilities.
5. The mentor demonstrates the kinds of behaviors, attitudes, and values that lead to success in the organization.
6. The mentor helps the protégé deal with difficult professional dilemmas.
7. The mentor supports the protégé and shows respect.
8. The mentor demonstrates personal caring that goes beyond business requirements.

Mentoring should not be confused with coaching. The following differentiation also comes from the Harvard business review book noted above:

Coaching	Mentoring
Goals are to correct inappropriate behavior, improve performance, and impart skills that the employee needs to accept new responsibilities.	Goals are to support and guide personal growth of the protégé.
The coach directs the learning and instruction.	The mentored person is in charge of his or her learning.
Though the subordinate's agreement to accept coaching is essential, it is not necessarily voluntary.	Both mentor and protégé participate as volunteers.
The focus is immediate problems and learning opportunities.	The focus is long-term personal career development.
The role is one of telling.	The role is heavy on listening, providing a role model, and making suggestions and connections.
Usually concentrates on short-term needs. Administered intermittently on an "as-needed" basis.	Long-term duration.
The coach is the coachee's boss.	The mentor is seldom the protégé's boss.

As a part of the requirements to be a Fellow in the American College of Healthcare Executives, I formally mentored a junior executive for six months. This was a formal relationship with agreed-upon terms, including how often we would meet and what we would accomplish. It was a beneficial relationship for both of us, and the terms of the agreement were met. In contrast I have many times had women write or say to me that I have been a mentor in their lives and have made a significant contribution to their development. In my experiences, the informal mentoring was probably as vital and significant as the formal mentoring even though I didn't recognize my role as mentor at the time of the informal mentoring. Because of that, I believe that informal mentoring involves the following:

1. There must be a modeling behavior congruent with our beliefs and organizational culture. Obviously, if my walk and talk had not been congruent, women would not have found that I was someone they would want to emulate and learn from.

2. There should be an approachability and openness to talk with others within and outside of the organization. An organizational culture of learning and trust and development of staff is a perfect petri dish for growth within an organization. Mentoring is all about guidance and teaching, which is really about growth of the individual. Out of growth of the individual comes growth of the organization.

3. There should be a willingness on the part of the mentee to show their vulnerability and on the part of the mentor to accept vulnerability without reproach, reprisal, and with some kindness.

Let me use the example of myself as a senior executive being mentored by a more senior executive, the CEO of my health system, Robert Milewski. This was not a formal relationship of mentoring; however, we met on an informal basis periodically for lunch, and during these meetings he would give me guidance on dealing with governance issues and handling particular board situations. Now, if his behavior on a daily basis did not exhibit a high degree of competence in handling governance issues, I would not have used his guidance, and he would have been an ineffective mentor. Also, if he was not approachable and open in his conversation with me and if we hadn't developed a trusting relationship, the mentoring would not have been effective. Because of that, I knew I could show him some of my vulnerability as a leader without fearing that he would assume I was incompetent in my leadership role. My relationship with him was such that I was able to grow with the guidance he gave me, and my organization was stronger as a result. Conversely, if I did not have him to mentor me in those situations, if I didn't feel confident in disclosing my inadequacies, I might have made costly governance errors, and the organization could have suffered as a result.

If there is someone you would like to have mentor you, ask them to be your mentor. No matter how busy you think they are, they will most likely find it a compliment, and they will make time to mentor you. Truly great leaders are leaders that give, and they love helping others to grow and develop and will welcome the opportunity to help a growing leader.

The second type of mentoring relationship is employee to employee, generally embarked upon between an established employee who has longevity in the organization and an employee just hired and joining an organization. I developed a mentoring program for my organization so that a new employee is mentored by an established employee, and I found it to be extremely successful. The mentors are volunteers and are chosen to become mentors based on their acclamation to the corporate culture, their work performance, and positive spirit. There is no extra pay to mentor, but being a mentor is positively reflected on their annual performance review. Each mentor-mentee relationship lasts six months, and during that time the mentor is reimbursed up to seventy-five dollars for expenses related to taking the mentee out for coffee or lunch or a celebratory graduation. In addition, I host a mentor lunch quarterly in a nice restaurant where we enjoy each other's company and look at what is working and not working in the mentoring program. Each new employee is assigned a mentor, and that mentor contacts them at orientation if possible or soon afterward. The object is to have a friend for the new employee, someone who is there as a resource, someone to orient them to the culture and customs of the organization, and someone they can trust to bounce off ideas, issues, and concerns. Not every mentor-mentee relationship is a good fit, and in those cases new mentors are assigned with no hard feelings.

Kathy Lacey in her book *Making Mentoring Happen* lists a lot of benefits to organization, mentor, and mentee with employee-to-employee mentoring programs. Mentors experience four key benefits:

- satisfaction in serving altruistically
- sense of being needed
- professional recognition
- increased self-esteem

The mentees have an improved overall performance while they gain access to the mentor's network, acquire skills and knowledge, and have higher job satisfaction than those employees who aren't mentored.

The organization is the really big winner because both mentor and mentee have increased

productivity, and they increase their work skills, leadership skills, and motivation. New talent within the organization is discovered. There is improved organizational communication and understanding, better recruitment and retention of staff, and lower staff turnover. Overall, what little funds you invest in a program like this will be well rewarded.

The third type of mentoring relationship is adult to young person. Even though I received mentoring as a young person and believe strongly in it, that type of mentoring is not my area of expertise. All of the information on mentoring a young person written here was obtained from Kristina Marshall, President and CEO of Winning Futures. Winning Futures is an award-winning nonprofit organization that makes a difference in the lives of young people. They offer school-based mentoring programs and workshops for middle school and high school students in southeast Michigan and are now implementing their model throughout the country. All of their programs focus on the life skills of character value identification, goal setting, career preparation, and strategic planning. A portion of the proceeds from this book will be donated to the Winning Futures organization, and you can learn more about the organization by going to their website at www.winningfutures.org.

I was very fortunate when I was a young person to have mentors around me that helped me along my life path. So many young people are not that fortunate. The presence of a strong, stable adult can dramatically increase the likelihood that a child will graduate, attend school regularly, create goals and career expectations, and grow to become a positive, functional adult. Without intervention by caring adults, youth can make choices that will negatively impact their entire lives. Students may become a drain on the local community because they are involved in criminal activities, do not graduate, and lack employability skills. A great way to give to your community and to help young people is to become a mentor, which you can do through your church or through an organization such as Winning Futures. Winning Futures is a school-based program in which mentors and students meet in classrooms during school hours and follow a structured curriculum. The program has experienced very high success rates. Mentoring takes place one time per week for one hour on a weekly or bi-weekly basis. On off weeks mentors and mentees interact through letters/e-mails, phone calls, and off-site meetings. Using the Winning Futures curriculum, facilitators provide a five-minute lesson, and mentoring teams complete related activities including group discussions, hands-on activities, written exercises, and student presentations. The adult mentors teach students life skills including budgeting, creating supportive relationships, resume development, career exploration, and academic, personal, and professional goal-setting and planning. Here are the amazing results:

- Ninety percent have pursued continuing education after graduation from high school.
- Eighty-nine percent after graduation are employed.
- Eighty-two percent have long-term goals, and of those, ninety-four percent have steps and a plan in place to reach those goals.
- Ninety-five percent have short-term goals, and of those, ninety-seven percent have steps and a plan to reach those goals.

In addition, graduates believe that the tools taught in Winning Futures helped them as follows:

- Set goals (88 percent)
- Achieve their goals (81 percent)
- Understand their values (83 percent)
- Be more prepared for their careers (86 percent)
- Work better with others (85 percent)
- Have a positive attitude (91 percent)
- Be more self-reliant (89 percent)
- Be more successful in life (89 percent)

There are wonderful stories about the young people helped through this organization, which you can hear about on their website at www.winningfutures.org. When you change the life of a young person, you not only change that life but the lives of generations to come. I hope you'll take the time to give your money or time to support a youth mentoring program.

Chapter Nine: Finding Balance in Your World

Probably one of the hardest things for a woman executive and leader to do is find balance in her life and world, and yet it is probably one of the most important. I wish I could tell you that I have always had balance in my life. One day when I came home from work, the kids came running out to greet me. As we walked up the steps to the house, they were literally peeling off my executive uniform. They wanted me out of work clothes and into "Mommy clothes." The profoundness of their action hit me like a two-by-four. They needed more of me. Another time, my daughter drew a picture of me with about four arms on each side of my body. I took the picture to my sister, a psychologist, for evaluation. She said that it showed I was "busy." I interpreted it as too busy. My kids not only needed more of me, they needed the part of me that wasn't busy doing the tasks of motherhood like making dinner and giving baths. They needed the fun, the singing, the reading, the sitting on the couch together. These two incidents happened not coincidentally right after we had built a new house, followed by my company building a large building to house our operations. When our office building was completed, we dedicated the building to my grandmother since she was our first patient and inspiration for the care we gave. And in the lobby of that building, we put a plaque of my grandmother and that commemorative dedication on the wall. I looked at that plaque, and it struck me then that someday the only remembrance of me in that building and that company would most likely be a plaque just like that. What would really be significant that I had left behind? What would really count out of all that I had accomplished?

What about me would I wish to have remembered? Would my legacy be that company and only that company? I realized then that as much as I loved what I was building in that company and as much as I wanted to be thought of and remembered as a great leader, what I wanted the most was the legacy of being a great mother, wife, and person. I wanted to be remembered as someone who was gracious and smiled easily. I knew that at that moment, I was not on the right track to accomplish that legacy. Right then, I permanently committed to living a balanced life. Not that from time to time I don't slip up—because I do. Not unlike the stock market, from time to time it is necessary to make a course correction in the balance of my life.

What does it really mean to live a balanced life? In the biggest picture, that view you might get when orbiting the earth; it is a balance between your work and non-work life. In that perfect world, you are able to give the amount of energy and creativity at work necessary to do well and accomplish your goals while having enough energy and creativity in your personal life as well. The right balance in these two areas will lead to success on both fronts and do a lot to get you that happy fulfilled life that you'd like to have. However, that's easier said than done because keeping balance between your work and non-work life isn't just about appropriating the right amount of time to each of these parts, though that's definitely a part of it. It's about doing the right things within your non-work life to make sure everything works.

Before we talk about what you need for your non-work life, let's talk a little bit about appropriating your time. Most of us go to work in the morning, fresh, and rearing to go. All of you that are or have been executives know that the work of an executive can really be endless. There is always something more you could do to improve, plan, motivate, monitor, create, and execute in your work world. And so often in an effort to do all those things and build that fantastic company, we keep doing, doing, doing, especially when we have energy and are in "the zone" at work. Often times, I did really great work after the end of the "official" work day when everyone else had gone home. So what happened? I would give the largest part of that day and then many more hours to work, and when I finally got home, I was short on time, short on energy, short on patience, and I would end up being a too-busy mom with no time for the fun stuff with my family. It is not unusual that we give the best part of our lives to the part of our life that will most likely only end up to be a plaque on the wall. There will be intermittent periods of time in your work when you must work the long hours and sacrifice the time you would spend balancing your life, such as when there is an urgent matter to be attended to or a crisis that needs to be handled. Those should be the exceptions, and because you've lived a balanced life, when those urgent situations occur, your family not only understands, but they also rally around to help you.

Now that we've talked about balancing time between the work and non-work life, let's look closer at what it means to balance your non-work life.

When we talk about balancing your non-work life, we now want to focus on you as an individual. To be balanced is to be a healthy individual physically, mentally, and spiritually. The three are so closely interwoven that it's difficult to discuss them separately, so we will discuss each area individually and then integrate them together. You might be thinking, *I thought you wanted me to be a better mother or wife or sister or whatever your relationships might be.* And indeed I do, but in order to be better in and with any relationship you are involved in, you first must take care of yourself as an individual. This might sound a little self absorbed, but it really isn't. If you don't take care of yourself first, you will not have enough left over to take care of anyone else. Remember, if Mama ain't happy, ain't nobody happy.

So let's first talk about taking care of your physical self. Taking care of yourself physically includes good nutrition, exercise, fresh air, and rest. We'll look at each area separately, and please keep in mind that while these items might seem elementary, it is surprising how frequently and without thought we tear down our bodies. I like to refer to our body as the body temple. It reminds me that this body that runs around all day is really the encasement for our spirit. If we don't take good care of our bodies, then we don't feel good, and when we don't feel good, nothing else goes well or is enjoyable. Taking care of our bodies is paramount to our success and happiness. So with that in mind, let's talk about taking care of our bodies.

First of all, we need to put good food into our bodies. From our food, whether good or bad, our bodies are fed and similar to an automobile; if you want great performance, you must put premium fuel in the tank. Every five years the US Department of Health and Human Services publishes Dietary Guidelines for Americans and recommends what we should be doing to maintain health. I use their guidelines as a good reference. There are wonderful books on the fine points of good nutrition, but for now these guidelines will let you know if you're on the right track. For a link that will take you to the most current US Department of Health and Human Services Guidelines, visit my website at www.cheriewhiting.com. Here is an abbreviated version:

1. Emphasize fruits and vegetables in your diet and choose a variety of them. Also emphasize whole grains and fat-free or low-fat milk and dairy products.

2. Eat lean meats, fish, poultry, beans, eggs, and nuts.

3. Keep your diet low in saturated fats, trans fats, cholesterol, salt, and added sugar.

Secondly, get enough exercise. Exercise will help you manage your weight, increase your mood, relieve stress, promote sleep if not done right before bedtime, and help you avoid chronic illnesses including diabetes, osteoporosis, and certain types of cancer. And, best of all, you'll just feel better. I like to follow the recommendations of the Centers for Disease Control and Prevention. Adults need at least one hundred fifty minutes of moderate-intensity aerobic activity every week and muscle-strengthening activities on two or more days a week that work all major muscle groups. Aerobic activity can include walking fast, water aerobics, riding a bike, playing tennis, or pushing a lawn mower among other things and can be for periods as short as ten minutes at a time. Muscle strengthening can be achieved by lifting weights, working with resistance bands, doing exercises that use the body for resistance like pushups, heavy gardening, and yoga. For an up-to-date list and complete recommendations, go to my website www.cheriewhiting.com to click on the link to the Centers for Disease Control and Prevention. Keep in mind that exercise in the fresh air and preferably in a natural setting is best and promotes physical and mental well being.

Thirdly, get enough rest. The benefits of rest and relaxation are broad and powerful. Rest restores our energy. We do not have an inexhaustible supply of energy. Each day we tap into that reservoir of energy, and so many times we push ourselves beyond our threshold, depleting ourselves of health and beauty and often our pleasing personality! Then without having enough rest, we go into the next day, again, pushing ourselves past the amount of energy we can afford to use. Before long we're not only tired, but we begin to break down physically and mentally, becoming sick and losing our creativity. We must take time to get enough sleep and to relax and do nothing. This will allow our energy battery to recharge and lead to more optimal health and the feeling of well being.

Rest repairs our bodies. It is during periods of sleep and rest that our bodies restore from the wear and tear of life that we place upon them. Our bodies are really programmed to self heal, and, given the chance, that is what they will do. Think about breaking a bone; while a skillful orthopedic physician may set the bone in order to align it properly, that physician cannot cause the body to heal—only nature can do that. Given the right environment, the body will attempt to heal itself, and one big part of that environment is rest.

Rest gives our minds a chance to recover. While resting is no guarantee that your mind will rest, there is much you can do to calm your mind and enhance rest and sleep.

Rest and relaxation come in different forms. One form of rest is actual sleep. You should get enough sleep to wake up refreshed in the morning and rearing to go. Another form of rest is while you're awake. Many of you reading this are like me—you're doers. We doers think we have to keep going, going, going, and this is really common among business owners, leaders, executives, and entrepreneurs; we're driven to do more. Take time to rest while awake. My favorite way to take this kind of rest is to lie on the couch and watch an old movie. Or sit in a comfortable chair in front of a fire and listen to beautiful music. Most importantly, let you mind and body rest. If you're worn out, tired, discouraged, overwhelmed, or can't solve a problem, it is a sign that you need to rest. And if you rest, you will recover and have all you need to accomplish what must be done and solve any problem you need to solve.

When I started my first business, I was blessed to be able to vacation frequently on the beach in Florida because my mother lived there. Those short rests where the kids could play in the sand and the waves lapping up on the shore soothed my nerves, made all the difference. It was also a place where I could recover and then get into the creative mode of planning for my company. So take little vacations as often as you need them, and remember they are necessities not luxuries.

Human beings were designed to need rest; that's why at creation, God set aside one day a week just to rest. Jesus says that "the Sabbath was made for Man, not Man for the Sabbath." I have been blessed to have kept one day of rest per week since I was born. This day of rest, which was commissioned at creation, is intended, I believe, to really save us from ourselves. What a blessing to rest our minds from our work for one day and spend that time with family; it has been a source of blessings for me physically, mentally, and spiritually. For more information on Sabbath rest go to the links on my website at www.cheriewhiting.com.

Important to remember here when thinking about balance is that to lead a happy and healthy life, we need work, play, and rest in the right proportions. You will get into a rhythm of work, play, and rest that will be best for you, and you'll know it's working because you will feel good!

We've talked about balancing your physical and mental life, but what about your spiritual life? In the western world, we often give too little significance to the fact that we are spiritual beings. We emphasize the body and the mind when really these are the parts of us that you can see and touch, and yet the biggest part of who we are is the part you can't see or touch, which is the spirit. It really started with creation and the fact that we were made in the image of God, and this image is spiritual. So in order to lead a balanced life, we must take care of our spiritual self—feed it in its own way. Our spirit is what gives us power and strength, creativity and energy, wisdom and personality. And the only way to have power and strength and creativity and energy and wisdom and personality in a positive, giving, and good way is to connect our mind with the mind of our Creator. This is the secret of having a powerful spirit. There are great books that explain this in much greater detail and much more convincingly than I can and that I have listed on my website www.cheriewhiting.com, but I recommend highly two books to get you started. The first is *The Bible* and the second is *The Science of Being Great* by Wallace D. Wattles. The closer you are to the source of all power, the more powerful you will become.

There are several things I would recommend you do to feed your spirit, and I've listed them below.

First, connect with God through meditation and prayer. This should be done daily and, even better, without ceasing.

Secondly, read inspirational reading. If you find yourself lacking spiritually, if you're poor in spirit or feeling discouraged, start reading inspirational books for a minimum of ninety minutes per day. I guarantee you it will change your mindset, and you will feel better. I have included a list of inspirational books for you on my website, some of which have made a huge impact on my life. I would also suggest that you stop reading newspapers and listening to the news. Nothing is as discouraging or disheartening as listening to news chosen for its sensational nature. There are lots of great and inspirational things happening in the world, but your chances of finding them on the news are almost nonexistent. Read good news and inspirational materials only!

Now you have an idea of what it takes to have a balanced life. I suggest that you keep what is important to you always before you. One way to do this is to have goals that you review frequently. These goals should include every part of your life and should include physical, mental, and spiritual goals as well as goals for family and work. When you make the goals, be sure they are representative of a balanced life, and then when you are reviewing your goals, it will be easy to see that you are out of balance if your goals aren't being realized in one particular area. Monitor yourself and make course corrections as necessary. As an intelligent leader and the only person responsible for you, it is up to you to make sure you are always on track and in balance, and you will be when you follow the simple suggestions in this chapter.

Chapter Ten: The Final Ingredient in Creating Your Own World

In the last nine chapters you have learned how you can define the world you want to create. Once that world is defined you now know how to create the environment. Then on that great foundation you will build your team of superstars. To differentiate yourself in the marketplace, you will commit to being passionate about service. And, you will become a strong and competent leader. With your company growing and thriving and reaping the rewards that comes with the world you're creating, you will make mentoring an important part of your business and life. Then in order to enjoy the world you're creating, you will make sure that you are living a balanced life. And yet with all these parts of the formula for successfully creating your own world, there is one ingredient missing. One ingredient that is still unidentified.

Remember that Albert Einstein quote about reality? So far your reality may have been that as a woman you can't succeed, you won't be able to accomplish all you've dreamed of, and you're not good enough or smart enough. I'm here to tell you that that is just an illusion. You *can* do and be anything that you wish. How? By believing in yourself and holding a positive mental attitude. That's the missing ingredient—believing you can and moving forward with a *positive mental attitude*. It's a simple idea yet hard because you have probably spent your life up to this time thinking the opposite. Changing your reality by changing how you think is probably the hardest task you will have to do, but you can do it!

I was very fortunate to grow up with people surrounding me who believed in me, so in turn I believed in myself. In addition, I had a strong belief in God and his relationship to me. For that reason, when I came up against obstacles like the bankers who didn't believe in me, the people I marketed who didn't take me seriously, and when I couldn't make payroll, I just kept moving forward. I pushed those moments of discouragement out of my mind. That may not have been your experience so far, and so I'm going to give you some steps to help you. I do all of these things myself and always have, yet reading one book helped cement these ideas for me, and I highly recommend that you buy this book immediately and start reading it: *Success through a Positive Mental Attitude* by Napoleon Hill and W. Clement Stone. Both Hill and Stone studied hundreds of the most successful people in the world, and they came to one single element that they all held in common; that element was a positive mental attitude. A positive mental attitude is the *one* essential ingredient to success. So I start my steps with that all important element:

1. *Hold a positive mental attitude.* Positive thoughts are comprised of thoughts of faith, joy, love, faithfulness, integrity, hope, optimism, courage, initiative, generosity,

tolerance, tact, and kindliness. I think we all probably know someone who is consistently negative. That person, who finds the negative in every situation and who becomes offended at the slightest provocation. Maybe, that person is you. It has been proven that like thoughts attract like thoughts, so thinking negatively only attracts more negative thoughts. The trick then, is to stop or limit all of your negative thoughts and turn them into positive thoughts. That might be very difficult at first and use a lot of your energy, but if you keep trying, you will find that it is easier and easier to think positive thoughts. Then, those positive thoughts attract more positive thoughts and you will find wonderful, positive things happening in your life.

Aim for high goals and constantly strive to achieve them. As Hill and Stone put it, and with which, I'm adding my own gender twist, "Anything the mind of a woman can conceive it can achieve with positive mental attitude."

2. *You can achieve anything you conceive if you have a positive mental attitude and if you are not violating the laws of man and God.* Anything gained when you go against the laws of man and God will not be lasting. When you follow the laws of man and God and think with a positive mental attitude, your actions will be blessed.

3. *Stay away from everything negative.* That includes the news. The media thrives on bad news, so that's what it feeds you. Look at what you need to and nothing more. Negativity does not serve you, nor does being around negative people. You need to surround yourself with positive people and people who believe in you and your dreams.

4. *You must push aside all doubts that you can achieve what you want to achieve.* You must never entertain thoughts of failure. Push aside all thoughts that you won't succeed, even when it seems irrational. You will need a lot of self talk. Tell yourself, this is just an illusion. My reality is success and only success!

5. *You must keep your vision always before you.* Tape it to your windshield, plaster it on your office wall, and put it on your bathroom mirror. Do whatever it takes to keep it clear in your vision.

6. *Read inspirational reading every moment that you can.* I have a bibliography on my website, www.cheriewhiting.com. When discouragement or negative thoughts push into my mind, I know that I need more inspirational reading. Gigi Graham, Billy Graham's daughter, has said that discouragement is Satan's calling card, and I believe it! And the way to combat that is inspirational reading and prayer.

7. *Remember that God is always a good God!* He wants to help you! Go to Him for help and wisdom and all good things. He will never let you down if you have faith and believe.

8. *Remember that life is a journey*. Enjoy all of life along the way.

9. *Be thankful and full of gratitude for everything and every person in your life.* Even be thankful for the struggles and difficulties as they are teaching you and refining you for this life you are creating.

You now have the formula for creating your own world. Go forth with faith and belief and energy in all you do, knowing that while you might not be able to change *the* world, you can certainly change *your* world. May God richly bless you.

References

Agor, Weston H. *Intuitive Management*. New Jersey: Prentice-Hall Inc, 1984.

Bass, Bernard M. *Stogdill's Handbook of Leadership*. New York: The Free Press, 1981.

DePree, Max. *Leadership is an Art*. New York: Bantam Doubleday Dell, 1989.

Eagley, Alice H. and Carli, Linda L. *Women and the Labyrinth of Leadership*. Harvard Business Review, 85(9), 62-71.

Gibbs, Nancy. What Women Want Now. *Time Magazine*, 174(16), 2009.

Harvard Business Essentials. *Coaching and Mentoring*. Boston: Harvard Business School Publishing, 2004.

Hill, Napoleon. *Think and Grow Rich*. Meriden, Conn: The Ralston Society, 1938.

Hill, Napoleon and Stone, W. Clement. *Success Through a Positive Mental Attitude*. New York: Simon and Schuster, 1960.

Robbins, Stephen P. *Organizational Behavior*. New Jersey: Prentice Hall, 2001.

Rowan, Roy. *The Intuitive Manager*. Boston: Little, Brown and Company, 1986.

Shea, Gordon, F. *Mentoring: A Practical Guide*. Menlo Park, California: Crisp Publications, 1997.

Vance, Mike and Deacon, Diane. *Think Out of the Box*. New Jersey: Career Press, 1995.

listen|imagine|view|experience

AUDIO BOOK DOWNLOAD INCLUDED WITH THIS BOOK!

In your hands you hold a complete digital entertainment package. In addition to the paper version, you receive a free download of the audio version of this book. Simply use the code listed below when visiting our website. Once downloaded to your computer, you can listen to the book through your computer's speakers, burn it to an audio CD or save the file to your portable music device (such as Apple's popular iPod) and listen on the go!

How to get your free audio book digital download:

1. Visit www.tatepublishing.com and click on the e|LIVE logo on the home page.
2. Enter the following coupon code: 932f-a60a-4a4f-07ee-6576-83f3-9a2b-b271
3. Download the audio book from your e|LIVE digital locker and begin enjoying your new digital entertainment package today!